ALIENology

Fred DeRuvo

ALIENology

Copyright © 2011 by Study-Grow-Know

All rights reserved. Written permission must be secured from the publisher to use or reproduce any part of this book, except brief quotations in critical reviews or articles.

Published in Scotts Valley, California, by Study-Grow-Know
www.studygrowknow.com • www.rightly-dividing.com

Unless noted, Scripture quotations are from The Holy Bible, English Standard Version®, copyright © 2001 by Crossway Bibles, a publishing ministry of Good News Publishers. Used by permission. All rights reserved.

Images used in this publication (unless otherwise noted) were created by the author, and are from clipartconnection.com and used with permission, ©2007 JUPITERIMAGES, and its licensors. All rights reserved.

All Woodcuts used herein are in the Public Domain and free of copyright.

All Figure illustrations used in this book were created by the author and protected under copyright laws, © 2011.

Cover design by Fred DeRuvo

Cover Image by: © innovari - Fotolia.com

Edited by: Hannah Richards

Library of Congress Cataloging-in-Publication Data

DeRuvo, Fred, 1957 –

ISBN 0983700605
EAN-13 9780983700609

1. Religion / Demonology & Satanism

ALIENology

Contents

Foreword: 5
Chapter 1: Knowing 7
Chapter 2: Alien Encounters 14
Chapter 3: Their Message 22
Chapter 4: Fourth Dimensional Living 36
Chapter 5: The Light that is Not 43
Chapter 6: Language of Aliens 49
Chapter 7: Who are They…Really? 53
Chapter 8: The Fallen 61
Chapter 9: Preparing for War 65
Chapter 10: Who is Satan? 73
Chapter 11: The Forces that Shape Us 85
Chapter 12: The New Age Alien 95
Chapter 13: Why the Message is Inviting 116
Chapter 14: Upcoming Scenarios 124
Chapter 15: Restoring What Was Lost 157
Chapter 16: What About You? 163

And no marvel; for Satan himself is transformed into an angel of light.

– *2 Corinthians 11:14*

FOREWORD

Years ago when I was growing up as a kid, it was not difficult to separate fact from fiction in the world of science. It was easy to understand and know that aliens were not real, but only existed in books and movies.

This is what we were told and how aliens were presented. They were often portrayed as malevolent, selfish creatures that would destroy humanity if it meant saving themselves. They liked our planet and had no qualms about tossing us out so they could move in.

Movies with this theme are still being made; however, another type of movie related to aliens has also become huge in the Sci-Fi world. Movies that portray aliens as either defenseless creatures or altruistic beings have garnered a growing audience.

It is not uncommon to see aliens as *benevolent*. They have good feelings, in spite of their superior intelligence and perceived aloofness. Though they often do things based on that intellect, they are not wholly devoid of compassion. In essence, they are often portrayed more as *angels* than aliens. Many movies today are created to cause people to make a connection – the connection between the angel of the Bible and the alien of science fiction.

This book has been written because of just how big the subject of *Alienology* (or the study of aliens) has become. People seem unable to get enough where aliens are concerned. These people tend to see aliens in terms of *super* humans. It's what people would *evolve* to if given half the chance.

To a growing number of people, aliens exist and are here to *help*. They want us to *achieve,* either because they have some sense of deep-seated concern for us or because they see our annihilation as affecting their existence, or because they themselves have a large stake in our destiny since many are coming to conclude that aliens *created us*. These are difficult things for the uninitiated to hear or read.

Could it be possible that not God, but aliens provided the spark of life that filled this planet with all manner of living forms? Many today think so, and it is for that reason that books like this need to be written.

For the purposes of this book, the terms *aliens, spirit guides, mediums, channelers, ascended masters,* and other esoteric labels are all used interchangeably. While many people see them as completely different, I do not. I see them that way. I will mainly use the term *aliens*, but the reader should know that I mean any type of entity that exists in the fourth dimension and sends messages of some type to us here, in our dimension.

When push comes to shove, it becomes clear that either the Bible has mistakenly appropriated what aliens have done, or aliens have attempted to mirror what the Bible teaches. If the former, then God does not exist as He is revealed through the Bible. If the latter, then the question must be asked: are aliens something *other* than aliens? Could they be demons masquerading as benevolent aliens?

Read on.

Fred DeRuvo, June 2011

1

Knowing

Only the chosen ones hear their voices. That was one of the lines Nicolas Cages' onscreen son Caleb said in the film *Knowing* just before he, along with a girl named Abby, joined the aliens to be taken to an unknown place, leaving his father and everyone else behind on this planet. Only the chosen ones hear the voices of the aliens. It reminds those of us who know the Scripture that *"many are called while few are chosen"* (cf. Matthew 22:14).

This particular movie is filled with many biblical references from the start without actually quoting the Bible. The movie itself portrays aliens first as seeming to have evil intentions with malevolence, while in the end are shown to be compassionate, despite their powerful abilities, which could be used to destroy humanity.

ALIENology

Nicolas Cage plays John, an astrophysicist, whose young son Caleb is given one of the envelopes from a time capsule at school that had been sealed fifty years prior at the same elementary school. The capsule contains many envelopes and inside those envelopes are drawings that children from 1959 made to be seen years later.

One particular student named Lucinda did not draw anything at all. Instead, her page contained rows and columns of numbers in no particularly noticeable order. Lucinda was a sad little girl, who stood alone during recess, staring into the sky and the sun.

She was always lonely, though never alone, because Lucinda always managed to hear the whispering of beings that no one else could see or hear; voices filtered through whatever other sound competed for her attention. Driving her to the brink of madness, it was as if she had already been captured by aliens. They certainly had her attention.

It was this page created by Lucinda that young Caleb took home with him, and it was this paper that John began to interpret, quite by accident.

The upshot of the story is that aliens have either *guided* our planet or have *known* what would befall it for generations. John was able to surmise that the paper containing the rows and columns of numbers connected with tragedies occurring on specific dates, at specific longitudes and latitudes, and detailed the number of dead. Looking ahead, John realized that the sun would give off a micro-tesla burst of heat that would cause a worldwide conflagration. Because of this, aliens had implemented a plan that would save the chosen of this planet.

These particular chosen individuals would be taken to another planet where life would start all over again. It would be hoped that this new venture, with children on a fresh new planet, would allow humanity to succeed. One can only imagine, but it is clear that for those who like to believe that aliens are the good guys, merely wanting to help humanity achieve what is normally thought to be impossible, they will have little difficulty believing it.

For those who have a more difficult time accepting the possible fact that aliens are altruistic, they will need more convincing elsewhere. However, the study of aliens or *Alienology* has persisted and even grown to an ever-increasing level so that now people believe that aliens not only exist, but *varieties* of alien races and cultures exist, each with their own goals. Just as the various cultures of human beings have varying goals, so too do aliens.

If you have done any study in this realm at all, you know that some aliens (we are told) are mainly good. Others are mischievous, while a few are malevolent or uncaring. In the movie *Knowing*, it is clear in the end that the aliens portrayed in the movie are indeed *good*, though initially, as has been stated, they certainly appear to have it in for human beings – or at least a select few.

Another thing to note about *Knowing* is the way in which biblical moments are interwoven throughout the movie. For instance, at one point, when John confronts one of the aliens demanding that they stay away from his son Caleb, the alien simply opens his mouth and an intensely bright light is emitted, momentarily blinding John.

As John struggles to see, he flails wildly around with his flashlight and staggers a bit because of his temporary blindness. This particular scene is reminiscent of what occurred with the account of Lot and the visiting angels in Sodom prior to its destruction.

Genesis 19 tells us the story of Lot's encounter with two angels who come to Sodom to take him and his family to safety. Why? Simply put, the Lord has decided to destroy both Sodom and Gomorrah for their sexual immorality.

As the two angels arrive in Sodom, Lot greets them and invites them to his home. Initially, the angels opt to remain out in the street for the evening, but Lot urges them to come to his home instead since it is not safe to be in the streets after dark.

The angels follow Lot to his home, but so did all the men in the city. The text tells us, "*But before they lay down, the men of the city, even the men of Sodom, compassed the house round, both old and young, all the people from every quarter: And they called unto Lot, and said unto him, Where are the men which came in to thee this night? bring them out unto us, that we may know them*" (Genesis 19:4-5).

My point is found in what happens *next*. While the men were trying to break down the door, Lot goes out and attempts to reason with these same men. This is certainly a risky move at best.

Having none of it, the crowd of men became even more obnoxious and stated that they would do what they wanted to Lot's visitors and then do something even worse to Lot. At this point, one of the angels reaches outside the door, pulls Lot in and closes the door.

Before he closes the door, though, the angel does something to the men. "*And they smote the men that were at the door of the house with blindness, both small and great: so that they wearied themselves to find the door*" (Genesis 19:11). Did you read that? The angels temporarily blinded the men so that they could not find the door. Notice though that the text says the men actually "wearied themselves" trying to find the door! These guys would not give up!

Was it merely coincidence that the movie *Knowing* included a scene that was reminiscent of the situation that occurred in Sodom? The alien temporarily blinded John in the movie, allowing the aliens to leave the vicinity without additional harassment. The angels in Genesis 19 temporarily blinded the homosexuals of the town in order to save Lot and leave the city without further incident.

There are other instances in which the aliens in the movie seemed more to resemble angels than aliens. As young Caleb and Abby joined the aliens to get on the ship that would take them to another planet, the aliens' human visages fell away, revealing their true form. This particular form looked like a combination alien and angel.

The aliens had what appeared to be glowing outlines for wings, though of course one wonders why they would actually need wings since they had a huge ship that carried them from place to place.

Those who have studied history and specifically ancient civilizations such as Egypt, the Mayans, and Aztecs, know that there are hieroglyphs and writings that seem to depict ancient space travelers. These travelers seem to have visited the people of ancient times. It is interesting to note that in at least some of these ancient depictions, these beings traveled from one place to another in some type of craft.

Certainly, in the movie *Knowing* these aliens are giving off mixed signals. Are they aliens or angels? Maybe they're something else altogether. They leave it to the audience to decide.

We also learn that Lucinda (who turns out to be Abby's grandmother) had become extremely interested in Ezekiel's description of the "*wheel in the sky*" (cf. Ezekiel 1:16). This was also some type of vehicle that had a wheel inside a wheel.

When the alien space ship finally shows up at the end of the movie, it lowers a sphere of sorts, which turns out to be a wheel within a wheel. It serves as an elevator to take the aliens and the two children above, to the waiting ship. Obviously, this was no accident.

The scene just before Caleb leaves the earth and his dad behind has Caleb assuring his father, John, that the aliens are *good*. They were there to protect them the entire time. However, for the audience, because these aliens never speak (except through telepathic whispers) and are virtually expressionless, they are seen more as malevolent creatures than anything else.

The movie ends with two important scenes:

1. *The earth is destroyed by fire, and*
2. *The children are seen running across a beautiful field toward a lone beautiful tree*

The earth being destroyed by fire is a recurring theme throughout the book of *Revelation*. In fact, there are a number of judgments where at least 1/3 of the earth is burned up by fiery judgments of God's wrath during the period known as the Tribulation.

Following the complete destruction of the earth in Revelation, God creates a new heaven and a new earth, and those who inhabit it have been purified. Never again will sin or suffering be part of that new world.

This is the intended ending for *Knowing*. While this earth is destroyed, the new "earth" that the children are taken to is brand spanking new, innocent, pure, and unadulterated. The two children are left there with other children to populate that new earth and hopefully create a better one than this current one.

Each of the two children is given one rabbit. The audience is left to assume that one rabbit is male, while the other is female. Other space craft have obviously dropped off other humans (probably other children, not adults) and it can be assumed that each child carries with him or her a different species of animal, one male and one female.

The new planet will become the new *earth*. The message, of course, is that aliens are our brothers and sisters, looking out for us and helping us when needed. It was also interesting to note that none of the aliens took on the form of *women*, also in keeping with the way the Bible reveals angels. There is never an instance of a woman angel in Scripture; only male angels.

The implied desire of the aliens in *Knowing* is to *help*, though initially, they appeared mysteriously vague and even slightly mean. From their vantage point, they see the trouble that this earth is facing and they also understand *how* the end will come and *when* it will come. They want to do something about it so that humanity is not completely destroyed.

Are they our friends? More importantly, is the movie telling us that they are actually our *creators*?

Let's see if we can find this same theme in other areas of *Alienology*...

2

Alien Encounters

The subject of alien encounters is one that is either believed outright by the zealous or seriously questioned by the doubter. There are pools of people who warmly receive whatever is stated by entities from other realms and dimensions as *truth*. These individuals firmly believe that aliens are here to do us a *favor*. They are seen as altruistic and loving.

Aliens, it is said, have been slowly revealing themselves to humanity in order to gain our trust. They seek to aid us through this very difficult period of our earthly history in order to bring us to a point of *self-sufficiency*, beyond wars, hatred, and especially the narrow-mindedness that is often revealed through a variety of religious endeavors. Many of these endeavors are described as *legalistic*.

Of course, it goes without saying that in all cases, Christianity is the single most attacked religion on the face of the planet. It is usually described by aliens as being completely misunderstood, and therefore, misappropriated.

Depending upon the type of alien that is doing the teaching, Jesus either *did* exist, but His reputation was completely blown out of proportion, or He did not exist and was merely a holographic image created by these higher beings in order to instruct us. Some aliens speak a great deal about the use of holograms as instruments of instruction for the human race.

In any case, the intended result is to *denigrate* Christianity and to cause the hearer(s) to doubt what they have always heard about Jesus and Christianity. It is interesting that people will question the Bible without mercy, in spite of any proof provided as to its veracity. However, when an alien being (who, by the way, is *never* asked or expected to offer proof as to his real identity) comes along and promotes the idea that Jesus was something else entirely, or that Christianity is merely the result of wishful thinking on the part of the original twelve, these words alone are sufficient enough to be accepted as *truth*. People sit in awe of these beings, hanging on every word, as messages are channeled through human beings to their audience, which waits with baited breath for new revelation.

What is equally troubling though is that people tend to believe what Hollywood produces, either consciously or unconsciously. In our first chapter, we discussed aspects of the movie *Knowing*, starring Nicolas Cage as John, an astrophysicist who comes into possession of a sheet of paper filled with rows of numbers that seemingly make no sense. John is able to break the code and begins to understand that major catastrophic events occurring on planet earth have either been simply known about or planned. In either case, the aliens have wanted to gain the attention of certain chosen ones on planet earth.

The reason aliens have decided to interfere by contacting chosen individuals is so that they can answer the call to be taken to another earth-like planet where life can begin all over again. Hopefully, all mistakes made on this planet will be left here to die with it.

The overwhelming question is: *why would aliens be concerned at all with what occurs on this planet?* The answer – though implied in the movie – is that these aliens either had a hand in creating (*seeding*) life on this planet to begin with, or *their* continued existence is somehow connected to humanity's continued existence. It has an evolutionary thread throughout in which all life is connected. It could also be that the producers of the movie simply wanted to portray aliens as *benevolent*, rather than *malevolent*.

If one recalls the history of alien movies and books since the early days of Hollywood, we learn that by and large, aliens were seen as diabolical, or even overtly evil. They came to destroy, to take over, and to push us out.

Think of the many movies from the 40s, 50s, and 60s. Movies like *Invasion of the Body Snatchers, The Beast from 20,000 Fathoms, The Day the Earth Stood Still, When Worlds Collide, The War of the Worlds,* and a host of other movies that portrayed aliens as villains.

Whether the movie had a *supernatural*, a *scientific*, or an *extra-terrestrial* overtone, it was clear that whatever came to earth, whether from underneath from the sea, or above from the skies, did so with evil intentions. Serials as far back as the 30s featured space ranger Flash Gordon fighting Ming the Merciless. In short, there was nothing good about alien life forms from these early days.

Over the passing decades, malicious aliens continued to exist in Hollywood, but they also began to portray decidedly good qualities.

ALIENology

The Queen Alien in the *Alien* trilogy starring Sigourney Weaver was simply a mother out to protect her hatchlings. Yes, that mother had acid for blood and jaws that split skulls, but ultimately, she was protecting what was hers and would stand for no interference from anything or anyone. Even humans will do that to protect their offspring.

Alongside these movies, films like *Star Wars* and a rebooted *Star Trek* made their way to the silver screens. These films showed that intelligent life forms existed beyond our solar system and they were not always bad. In fact, in some ways, the bad was clearly delineated from the good. "The Force" has become a phrase that is part of the vernacular of everyday language and mirrors what is taught within aspects of the New Age movement.

As time has marched on, aliens have become more human-like, with emotions, design, and superior intelligence. *If only we would trust them*, is their message. To this end, aliens have taken on forms that we can understand and appreciate. They stoop to our level so as not to frighten us. They simply want to be friends, or at least to gain our trust so that we will be able to discern the intelligence of their *plan*.

Like parents who chide their children and even keep certain things hidden from them because of the child's inability to comprehend it, so too do aliens do what is necessary for our growth, though we fail at times to truly comprehend *why* they do *what* they do. As children who place their trust in parents, so too should we abandon doubt in order to trust the direction that the aliens seem to be taking us.

Because of the fact that alien abductions by their nature are often harrowing, leaving the abductee with severe trauma, aliens have attempted to portray themselves as doctors and scientists, simply doing what they have to do to achieve their purposes for humankind. Because of this, alien abductions have become much more readily accepted in many circles today. The fear factor that is usually involved in alien abductions is dissolving and there are actually folks who *seek* to be abducted.

Of course, alien abductions can still be frightening, as much of the testimony from abductees explains. However, since these aliens are now seen as physicians and scientists, what was once extremely fearful is now becoming much more passively accepted.

In spite of all the movies that portray aliens as hellions from outer space out to destroy, there has never been a recorded incident of aliens attempting to do this on this planet. For the most part, aliens are seen as *observing* our planet and the situations that evolve. They are portrayed as needing to step in when necessary to either correct things that may destroy the earth if left unchecked, or to simply help us gain access to the next *spiritual* level.

It is the latter reason that is discussed most today. Aliens are good and want only the best for us. To this end, they endeavor to step in only when absolutely necessary to help us arrive to a spiritual plane that they themselves once stood at eons ago.

What we often mistake as malevolence, then, is in truth their way of helping us achieve. We mistake their help for hindrance, simply because it has taken so long to get to know them.

Even in many cases of alien abductions, the tremendous fear experienced by the abductee is generally seen as an overreaction to the *unknown*. Many abductees speak of being immobilized and completely unable to move, yet able to feel things acutely, while hearing (through telepathy) the thoughts of their alien abductors.

Being literally yanked out of their beds and into a place that appears to be cold, sterile, and alien, while being poked and prodded by alien creatures, is enough to cause any normal human being to become carried away with abject fear. These types of situations, whether real or in the mind's eye, are intense and therefore completely realistic and altogether unknown. Since the abductee has no frame of reference for the event, fear speaks loudly and clearly. Of course, the fear of *future unknown* also plays a large part in these abductions. What is the intent of these aliens? Are they friendly? How is that measured with beings that show little to no emotion? What will they do once the examination is completed? Will I be different? Will I remember this event? Will I have nightmares that are as vivid as the event itself? Will they return to abduct me *again*?

All of these questions speed through the mind of the abductee with no corresponding answer. At the very least, it leaves the abductee unnerved and vulnerable. At worst, it creates an abductee who becomes schizophrenic.

If history tells us anything, we can clearly see that alien abductions have become much more normalized in society today. We realize that over many decades, alien abductions, like out of body experiences, have taken on a sense of credibility that was lacking when they first began in the United States.

With everything that is being written about aliens and with the way they are being portrayed now in Hollywood, the question must be asked: *what is the truth and is there any way to determine what that truth is in the end?*

We must not forget to include beings that are commonly referred to as "ascended masters" or "spirit guides." Though these are often unseen even to the person who channels their messages and ideas to humanity, they are still in some form *alien* life to humans on this planet.

We normally think of aliens in terms of space beings piloting spacecraft or possessing some way to transverse space and possibly even time without a craft. One of the things that many aliens allegedly do is use telepathy to engage their subject's mind. It is through this ability that many books have been written by those who claim to have friends in the alien world, or other dimensions.

This author has been contacted by several individuals who have claimed to be channelers for beings from other dimensions. It normally follows that they insist that what they are doing is biblical and the beings they deal with only have good intentions for the world. They point out that statements made in my books or on my blog are very narrow-minded and judgmental.

When asked to provide proof of their claims and proof of the identity of the beings who channel messages to them, they are unable to do so and say as much. They indicate that it is impossible to know who the beings *truly* are, but since their message is one of comfort and love, then to question their motives is unnecessary as the message speaks for itself, regardless of the source of that message.

Is that true? Are we to simply take as truth any thought, word, book, or movie that comes to us if it *appears* to have some semblance of truth to it and if it is delivered with an attitude of compassion and peace? It would seem that we do not do this with other human beings, yet we are being told that we should not hesitate to do this with aliens.

In this author's mind, there is virtually no difference between an alien who abducts someone and plants ideas or concepts in their mind and an ascended master who does the same using some type of telepathy. How can there be any difference if the messages are fundamentally the same? Only the source and circumstances are different, but how are we to know that aliens cannot create images that appear extremely realistic? In short, we do not.

Whether they are ascended masters, aliens, higher beings, spirit guides, or whatever else they are called, the message is essentially the same. Only the delivery of that message and the circumstances surrounding that delivery are different from one person to the next.

In the end, then, are we really dealing with aliens, ascended masters, higher beings, or something else entirely? Is that simply how they refer to themselves, or what they encourage us to believe? It seems that all too often, what we call them does not matter, and they say as much. It is the *message* that we need to grasp, live by, and share. The message they present will open doors that our subconscious will create. All that is needed is to walk through those doors they unlock into that reality they describe. We are told that people are too often imprisoned by their own lack of creativity; that we have long given up on the idea that gods can *create*. It is the aliens' job to reunite us with this "gift" of creation in order to make this world a better place.

Ultimately, the world becomes better and evolves to its next spiritual level when all human beings grasp the same *goal*. Those who won't or are unable to do so will find themselves moved out of the way so that this planet can survive and master itself. Have you ever heard of the "great evacuation"? We will cover that later on in this book.

3

Their Message

Maybe it's just me, but it appears as though there is essentially *one overriding* message that emanates from the alien world, but which is transmitted in *numerous* to human beings in many different ways. While there seems at times to be many messages that are routinely bandied about from the alien world to this one, few seem to realize that some messages within the overall message are contradictive in nature. It is as if people hear what they want to hear and toss out anything that does not agree with their preconceived notion of what aliens are like and what they want us to know.

The point is that any number of messages emanate from the alien world; however, all are under one main heading. It all depends upon what alien is making the statement and from what branch of alien or culture he allegedly hails.

The generalized message from the alien world is essentially the same. It is their hope and desire to bring humanity to a higher level of existence. This is accomplished, they say, by helping human beings unlock their true potential. Inwardly, we are told, human beings are already gods. We possess everything that is needed to achieve whatever our minds can conceive. This one main message is fine-tuned by various other-worldly entities depending upon the specific humans or groups of humans to which they are relating their ideas.

Throughout this book, it must be realized that many movies and books have been produced and published that do not speak of or refer to aliens specifically. However, they do refer to and illuminate other *dimensions*. *The Matrix* trilogy is one such vehicle that introduced people to an "awake" world and a "dream" world. In that scenario, people actually existed in huge vats of chemicals that allowed the electricity their brains produced to be harvested and used by aliens of a type. They were actually machines that had outgrown the need for human beings except as a source of energy.

Human beings, while asleep in their own chemical vat, lived a life that seemed in all respects to be fully real to them. They were only dreaming, however, and yet the vividness of their dreams rivaled anything in reality.

It was when they began to fight their dream world, while fully involved in their dream reality, that they learned of the ability to move out from their dream world by waking up to their actual reality. Together, with other humans who woke up from their dream state, they became one in thought and goal. The goal was to overcome the machines that were simply using human beings for their own purposes.

At the end of the first Matrix movie, Neo (the main character who woke to the reality that he had been asleep and dreaming his entire life) looked at the viewer and essentially said that the future was wide open. Each person has the ability to create for themselves what they wished to create. They did not have to go along with their given existence.

So while *The Matrix* series did not deal specifically with aliens, it dealt with one of the main messages that aliens subscribe to; that all human beings are inherently gods. We were born/created that way and merely need to wake ourselves up to that reality. If they can be of service to us in that regard, they will certainly help. This is why they are waiting in the wings and over time have been slowly impacting society by making their presence known.

It is important to understand that regardless of whether or not people believe in aliens, gods, or simply the idea that humanity has the power to create reality, the truth of the matter is that the message is the same. The only thing that changes from one person to the next may be in *how* the message is delivered and who it is that delivers it. It all depends upon the individual's circumstances.

Those deep within the area of *Alienology* tell us that these aliens do not wish to impose themselves on humanity. The aliens realize of course that some people have a very difficult time believing in them while others would be seriously afraid of their presence because of "bad press" from prior decades. In those cases then, they choose to present their message in a far less intrusive and shocking way.

But what is less shocking: seeing an alien face-to-face and being taught that you are a god, or merely coming to that conclusion through what appears to be a fairly innocuous form of New Age thought? True, there are many human beings who welcome the idea of friendly and benevolent aliens. They look forward to such events. Many others cannot handle that idea and cast it off as nonsense.

Being sensitive to the various ways of interaction with human beings, aliens – it is said – want only what is best for humanity. Because of this, they are content to remain in the shadows until such a time when they can come out into the open without shocking the multitudes of human beings on this planet.

What is most interesting is that since the Wikileaks situation came to the fore, many documents have literally been purposefully leaked to the public which heretofore were classified and kept out of the public eye. A number of these documents deal with the alien phenomenon and the alleged fact that contact has been made.

If governments have indeed (allegedly) made contact with extra-terrestrials, then this would add some credibility to what the aliens have to tell us. The fact that governments have resisted telling the general population about aliens ties in with the aliens' stated agenda to not cause undue stress on people before they are able to allow as many people as possible on this planet to become used to the idea that they exist and want to help.

If the basic message given by aliens has to do with the alleged truth that human beings are already gods and can create their own realities, then what are the *other* sub-messages?

Normally, all the other messages have to do with *religion*. In fact, there is a plethora of supposed channeled messages from aliens and ascended masters that have to deal with religion, and few of them are complimentary toward Christianity specifically.

Even in those messages that at first appear to be positive where Christianity or Jesus is concerned, reading between the lines points out that even in their attempts to position themselves in favor of

Christianity or Jesus they wind up denigrating it. However, even here they do so *gently*, not meaning to create antagonism and anger against Christianity or Jesus (or Christians), but merely to unlock the truth about these things.

The more messages that are read and studied from various sources, the clearer it becomes that the agenda of aliens is to ultimately *deny* the tenets of Christianity by explaining it away. Some aliens can be downright brutish when it comes to their explanation of Jesus and what has become known as Christianity. Others are far more diplomatic.

The aliens are careful not to poke fun of or degrade something that people hold dear. However, they wind up doing this because of the way in which they attempt to explain it away. Normally, though, they are dealing with people who have little to no real attachment to the Bible or Jesus, so to these individuals, being able to see the "truth" once and for all is very freeing for them.

Alice Bailey (1880-1949) is credited with having written many books, most dictated to her from her *spirit guide*, the Tibetan (also known as Djwal Khul, or DK). Her books are studied by New Age aficionados today as they were just after first being published.

Some of her more well-known books are *The Externalization of the Hierarchy* and *The Reappearance of Christ*. Heavily involved in the Occult, what she learned, wrote about, and taught became the foundation upon which today's New Age movement was built.

Her spirit guide – The Tibetan – was prolific, as can be imagined. He presented himself as a humble individual (from Tibet) merely wanting to share his knowledge with Bailey in order that she might share that wealth of information with the world. How wonderful of him, wasn't it?

What is interesting about Bailey's messages, as well as messages of others before and after her, is that there are similarities between the messages. Apart from the denigration of Jesus and Christianity, there always comes a point where Jews are put down in some way. In other words, fault is always placed at the feet of the Jews for many of the ills in this world, as well as the perceived ills from which they themselves apparently suffer. They are seen and described as individuals who are unable to assimilate themselves into society and because of that inability they have created problems in the world that can only be solved by either helping Jews change, or by eliminating them altogether.

Of course, many alien/spirit guides don't put it like this. Instead, they imply that some cataclysmic event of the future will take care of the "problem" and will deal not only with the Jews, but with others who find themselves unable to go along with the program. This generally references *Christians*.

The Tibetan shows a bit of this in many of his messages to Bailey. In his case, he is careful to not overtly malign or belittle Jesus. He states he is *lower* than Christ. That much is certainly true. *"The Christ, Whom I serve as a disciple, and the spiritual Hierarchy, of which I am a member, are drawing steadily nearer to humanity; in the past I have used the statement to reassure you, 'The Hierarchy stands'; today I say to you, 'The Hierarchy is near'."*[1] This statement is from Bailey's *Externalization of the Hierarchy* and was written in 1946. Of course, while it is true that the Tibetan is lower than Christ, he does not serve Him...*willingly*. He serves Him because he must. He has no choice in the matter. This he conveniently leaves out.

The Tibetan goes on to enlighten Bailey as to the work that he says must be accomplished in the next several decades (*from 1946*).

---

[1] http://www.bibliotecapleyades.net/sociopolitica/externalisation/exte1276.html

1. **Prepare men for the reappearance of the Christ.** *This is your first and greatest duty. The most important part of that work is teaching men - on a large scale - to use the Invocation so that it becomes a world prayer and focuses the invocative demand of humanity.*
2. **Enlarge the work of the Triangles** *so that, subjectively and etherically, light and goodwill may envelop the earth.*
3. **Promote ceaselessly the work of World Goodwill,** *so that every nation may have its group of men and women dedicated to the establishing of right human relations. You have the nucleus, and expansion must be undertaken. You have the principle of goodwill present throughout the world; the task will be heavy indeed but far from impossible.*
4. **Undertake the constant distribution of my books, which contain much of the teaching for the New Age.** *In the last analysis, the books are your working tools and the instruments whereby you will train your workers. See that they are kept in steady circulation.*
5. **Endeavor to make the Wesak Festival (at the time of the May Full Moon) a universal festival** *and known to be of value to all men of all faiths. It is the festival in which the two divine Leaders, of the East and of the West, collaborate together and work in the closest spiritual union; the Christ and the Buddha use this festival each year as the point of inspiration for the coming year's work. See that you do likewise. The spiritual energies are then uniquely available.*
6. **Discover the members of the new group of world servers,** *whenever possible, and strengthen their hands. Look for them in every nation and expressing many lines of thought and points of view. Remember always that in doctrine and dogma, and in techniques and methods, they may differ widely from you, but in love of their fellowmen, in practical goodwill and in devotion to the establishing of right human relations they stand with you,*

they are your equals, and can probably teach you much.[2]
(emphasis added)

Since the time of this message, many have come to the conclusion that some type of "Christ" or Messiah *will* return. This is most clearly seen today with Islam, though the New Age movement has within it strong factions that have been proclaiming the coming Christ for years. For Islam, this Christ is referred to as the *Mahdi*. For the New Age movement, he is *Maitreya*.

Triangles are seen everywhere today. From the sides of the great pyramids to the symbols on the paper money of the United States and other countries, triangles symbolize the New World Order's power and unity. A triangle is created when three thoughts converge. The triangle is the symbol of universal divinity.

Triangles can also be formed with human beings. It happens when groups of three individuals come together as a unit within New Age or other esoteric circles to bring goals to fruition. "*International participants 'sit quietly for a few minutes and link mentally with other members of their triangle, or triangles. They invoke the energies of light and goodwill, visualizing theses energies as circulating through the three focal points of each triangle and pouring through the networks of triangles surrounding the planet. At the same time they repeat the Great Invocation and so help to form a channel for the downpouring of light and love into the consciousness of humanity'.*"[3]

The Great Invocation is what the proponents of New Age and modern Occultism recite as prayer through meditation as often as possible. While it *appears* to be Christian, it is far from it. Let's take a moment to look at the entire invocation and break it down from there. This will allow us to see it for what it is; Christian or not.

---

[2] http://www.bibliotecapleyades.net/sociopolitica/externalisation/exte1276.html
[3] http://www.lucistrust.org/en/service_activities/triangles

From the point of Light within the Mind of God
Let light stream forth into the minds of men.
Let Light descend on Earth.

From the point of Love within the Heart of God
Let love stream forth into the hearts of men.
May Christ return to Earth.

From the centre where the Will of God is known
Let purpose guide the little wills of men –
The purpose which the Masters know and serve.

From the centre which we call the race of men
Let the Plan of Love and Light work out
And may it seal the door where evil dwells.

Let Light and Love and Power restore the Plan on Earth.[4]

This, of course, should **_not_** be used as a prayer by anyone, much less an authentic Christian, because the *god* that is being prayed to is not the God of the Bible, but the god of this world, *Satan*. The more people there are who come together to pray this prayer, the greater the door opens for Satan to enter into their lives and impact society.

The message then of these spirit guides is one which seeks world unity – or *oneness* – in the hopes that the people of this world will come to realize their true spiritual destiny. Whether these ascended masters, aliens, or spirit guides ever mention some form of god is beside the point. They can get the exact same message across *without* ever having to mention God. For the atheist or agnostic, the message can be truncated so that only the part about creating reality is revealed. Other words can be used in place of "god(s)," or "divinity," etc., without losing the meaning of the intended message.

---

[4] http://www.lucistrust.org/en/service_activities/the_great_invocation__1

For those who are *religious* and even believe they are Christians, the channeled message will come as fully religious. There are too many people in this world who do not know their Bibles at all. They are unable to discern truth from error and make no effort to find out.

Because of this lack of knowledge of God's Word, people are too often deceived with religious-sounding words and orthodoxy. The verbiage used in the above-quoted Great Invocation points this fact out.

We know from Scripture that there is a plan that all *fallen beings* ascribe to and wish to share (read: *brainwash*) with humanity. They want as many human beings as possible to think the actual plan of God as referenced in the Great Invocation *is* truly God's plan for this planet.

In fact, what aliens have disclosed to humans is what they call *The Plan of God*, and it was revealed to the world by Alice A. Bailey in 1936. Essentially, the Plan revealed by Bailey has to do with humanity's ability to conform to the values and ideals of the *coming new world order*.

Once these values and ideals are securely implanted within each individual, the individual will then be able to live in the *fourth dimension*. This is no mean feat. In other words, what we long to see, but cannot now see, we *will* see and experience, provided we are able to expand our consciousness enough to adopt the values and ideals of the world of the fourth dimension. This completes itself through our ability to live *divinely*.

"The only human beings who ever really help to save the world are those who can first take hold of themselves and live divinely. This is an

age of mind, and the use of the power of the human mind is the outstanding characteristic of our time."[5]

The carrot is being held just above the heads of all human beings. The belief that human beings can attain to life in the fourth dimension just as The Tibetan, ascended masters, spirit guides, and aliens do, is within humanity's reach, but we will have to work for it to make it happen. This is what we are being told and this is what we are to believe. Questioning it will simply forestall the results.

One must ask, aside from the obvious ability to float and flit from one dimension to another, what is so great about living fourth dimensionally? According to the Tibetan, living in such a way is equal to living *divinely* all the time. Who does not want to live divinely? Who does not want to be *god*? That's really what it all boils down to, doesn't it? It's what was offered and accepted by Eve and Adam and from that point onward, the only Person who ever *rejected* that offer was Jesus Himself. Thank God for that...*literally*.

How is living fourth dimensionally achieved? The answer is simple, though the technique used is not. *"For this great transition there is a technique of training marked by definite stages of progress and this new consciousness is to be achieved in the light of the soul by the power of the mind."*[6] If we sift through the pontificating, what we learn is that in order to make the full transition from where humanity is *now* to where it *needs* to be, the *power of the mind* must be fully activated. Once each person begins to understand and use this principle, he/she will come in contact with divine *love*. Who does not wish to be loved? Who would not wish to be loved *more* than they currently may be? Ultimately, who does not wish to actually *be* love? God is love, but at best, we are merely a reflection of His love under the best

---

[5] http://www.lucistrust.org/en/books/the_beacon_magazine/reprinted_from_the_beacon/the_coming_kingdom

[6] Ibid

possible circumstance. That circumstance will occur only with authentic Christians in the afterlife, when all vestiges of the sin nature have been removed.

The Plan of God as stated by the esoteric is to become gods ourselves, able to live divinely 100% of the time, floating to and from the fourth dimension at will. Once the power of the mind is released, the full universe begins to open up to those who have been closed off from it.

As the Tibetan continues to preach, he tells us that the Plan of God is worked out through **goodwill** to all humankind. *"We must let our personal feelings go in order that this wonderful plan may be materialized. There is no time for quarrel. There is no time for dividing ourselves off from one another because of fancied superiorities.* **There is only time to serve our fellowmen**. *It does not matter what nation we have been born into,* **we are one under God**. *Mankind with all its powers stands today on the verge of coming in contact with another aspect of the fundamental and divine principle of love. When that divine principle of love is wedded to the divine principle of intelligence we shall have appearing on earth the fifth kingdom of nature. This is the spiritual kingdom of nature.* **This is the spiritual kingdom of God wherein we shall function as Souls whose nature is love and wherein we shall demonstrate that love intelligently**."[7] (emphasis added)

So what is the problem with this message? In fact, *is* there a problem with it? Unfortunately, there is truth mixed with error. Yes, this world is under *one* god and according to the Bible, Satan is the prince of this world and the prince of the powers of the air. As God allows, Satan controls all that this world contains (cf. Ephesians 2:2; 5:8; 6:12; John 12:31).

---

[7] http://www.lucistrust.org/en/books/the_beacon_magazine/reprinted_from_the_beacon/the_coming_kingdom

Recall that when Satan tempted Jesus in the wilderness, he (Satan) offered Jesus all the kingdoms of this world (cf. Matthew 4). At no time did Jesus argue with Satan about ownership. He recognized that Satan was the owner (though not the rightful one) of this planet.

Refer again to the quote above and note the last sentence that I have bolded. Read it twice. If that isn't the most pained gobbledy-gook jargon, I don't know what is, do you? "...*wherein we shall demonstrate that love intelligently*." What, pray tell, does *that* mean? It's like trying to discern the meaning of the ramblings of a politician. They speak in platitudes and they say essentially *nothing*, though they are masters at saying the kind of things that people want to hear.

Our current president says one thing and does another, yet people continue to applaud his speeches. Most recently, because of the current situation in Libya, the UN voted to create a no-fly zone over Libya. Soon, Mr. Obama was on the TV (from Brazil, loaning them money for offshore oil digs), telling the world that the U.S. would have primarily an *advisory* role in the situation.

Within a day, war planes and jets were flying over Libya dropping missiles. In fact, it appeared that the U.S. was leading the way. Several days later, Mr. Obama stated that he was confident that he would be able to hand off the actual military movement to others, while the U.S. *went* to an advisory role.

The problem of course is that Mr. Obama had no backing from Congress to enter into a war situation (which is why it was called a "kinetic military action"). Further, he seems to have lied about the U.S. involvement.

This is the problem with politicians. Most of them say what they need to say to scratch people's ears. They seem intent on doing whatever they want to do for their own expedient gains.

This is exactly what aliens are doing, in my view. It must be *proved* that aliens have the best interests of human beings at heart. If that cannot be proven, then why should they be believed? The people who trust them implicitly seem like the same individuals who support politicians in spite of their lying, their double talk, and their insincerity. People like that are easily taken in because they go by the way things make them *feel*. Is there a problem with that? There certainly is, and it is the very thing that aliens seem to capitalize on in order to break down the natural resistance that is seated within human beings.

4

Fourth Dimensional Living

Living in the *fourth* dimension. It's what Marty had consistent problems with in the movie trilogy, *Back to the Future*. You'll recall Doc Brown telling Marty, "*You're not thinking fourth dimensionally, Marty!*" to which Marty would respond, "*Yeah, I have a tough time with that,*" or something similar.

The Plan of God, according to Lucis Trust (founded by Alice A. Bailey) and the New Age movement, is to hasten humanity's graduation from our *current* level of existence to the *next* level of existence. The next level is what they term *fourth dimensional living*. Fourth dimensional living is living as God lives. Only God or His created spirit beings can traverse from the third dimension to the fourth and back again. Who does not want to be able to do this?

The trouble with *The Plan of God* as explained by occultists and New Agers is that it is done through *self-effort*, for one. Additionally, the meaning of Christian-sounding terms is completely different, leading people to believe that they understand the meanings because they've heard them so often, when in point of fact, a new meaning has been applied. This is no different from dealing with people in cults. They often use Christian-sounding terms and phrases, but their meanings are far removed from orthodox or original meanings.

The Plan of God is a plan that is based on *works* and *deception*. Man is led to believe through deceptive means that he must work toward a type of salvation. This salvation is found allegedly within the realm of *fourth dimension living*. Humanity individually and collectively puts in the effort through meditation and acts of goodwill toward other human beings, animals, and the earth. As more people become completely enmeshed in the concept of spiritually meditating for world peace and love, as well as actually physically involving themselves in the process by doing good works for other people, the world moves toward that stage where people will become divine and live fourth dimensionally.

This can only occur when all people unite as one. With one mind, one purpose, and one vision, all people can do together what Nimrod failed (due to God's direct intervention) to do in Genesis 11. Nimrod – a hunter of men – was the world's first dictator, if you like. He was so passionate about what he wanted and worked so hard to bring all people together in one purpose that had God not intervened, it is clear from the text of Genesis that Nimrod would have achieved what he set out to achieve.

We are living in 2011 and yet the message that is being channeled from the fourth dimension to us is as old as Nimrod. Little if anything has changed.

All around us, books, movies, conferences, and more teach us that we must unite. The world is becoming smaller due to technology. We see a tsunami off the coast of Japan *as it happens*. We see and vicariously experience the destruction of that same tsunami on the upper portion of Japan.

We are constantly being told through a variety of sources that if we do not unite under the banner of one purpose, we will be lost. In essence, then, people are being told that the path to God is actually done without going *through* God. Why would we need to *go* to God if we are actually already gods? That would be a bit redundant, wouldn't it?

In the New Age movement, Lucis Trust, or any group like it, there is no need for a deity that is separate from the individual. This message, spread throughout humanity by the various channels already mentioned, intones that our divinity lies inherent within us. There is no need to actually seek this outside one's self. In fact, it is through meditation that we withdraw *into* ourselves to unlock and unleash the power of our own divinity, guided by the power of our mind that brings us to the realization that we are gods and helps us create that reality that will benefit all of mankind.

What Satan has always done is attempt to find a way that circumvents God. In the record of his sin (Isaiah 14 and Ezekiel 28), Satan strove to become God himself; to, in fact, take God's place. Succumbing to his own beauty and intelligence, he could not deal with the fact that he was a *created* being and would never be anything but *created*. This knowledge ultimately fueled the jealousy that Satan (Lucifer before his fall) harbored with an animosity that grew with each passing moment of time.

That animosity led him to openly rebel against God, taking 1/3 of the angelic host in that same rebellion. Lucifer could not overcome or overthrow God. He found out the hard way, yet continues that same work as Satan, the being who delights to devour those on earth (cf. 1 Peter 5:8).

The *Plan of God* as seen by those within the occult, the New Age movement, and other esoteric societies is a plan that is actually devoid of the God of the Bible. God has been avoided at all costs, being replaced by the god of this world.

What we are hearing today is no different from what Satan (through the serpent) stated to Eve. He told her then that once she ate of the forbidden fruit, her eyes would be open and she would be like a god. Satan plied her with promises of divinity.

There is some evidence to suggest that prior to the fall, Adam and Eve lived fourth dimensionally. We think of Adam and Eve merely being the perfect human specimens. Certainly, God would not create something that was below par. Adam and Eve looked human enough, talked as humans, thought as humans and did the things that human beings today do. However, up until the time that sin was found in them, they did all these things without sinning.

Once they sinned, things changed...*drastically*. There is the possibility that when Adam and Eve fell, the reason they opted to create clothing for themselves was due to the fact that there was something about their nakedness that created *panic*.

This led to the desire to cover their nakedness. But consider that while they may have been embarrassed to see one another naked, had they simply been naked prior to the fall they would merely be seeing each other *differently*, but outwardly, they would essentially still be the same. What changed would have been their *perspective*.

Consider though that maybe what changed was *more* than their perspective. Chuck Missler seems to come to the possible conclusion that both Adam and Eve may have been covered with some form of *light*. When they fell, that light went out. They realized that they were not only naked, but they were *missing* something entirely.

Missing that something is what caused them to feel that what they were previously "wearing" had to be replaced since it was no longer there. Thus, they quickly made clothing out of leaves.

When God finally entered the picture after the fall, one of the first questions He asked them was, *"who told you that you were naked?"* after hearing Adam admit that they hid from Him because they were afraid and naked (Genesis 3). After hearing Adam's and Eve's story (the serpent remained silent), God pronounced judgment.

Following the pronouncement of judgment, God then made clothing from some of the animals in the garden. I'm going to assume they were the type of animals that would later be used as sacrifices. With the skins of the animals, God created suitable clothing for Adam and Eve.

It seemed as though God was agreeing with Adam that the two needed to be *re-covered* because they had lost their original covering. Of course, God could have made the clothing because of the weather as well, knowing it was going to change.

Is this far-fetched? Not really, if we consider the fact that angels often appear in Scripture shining *brightly*. There is something uniquely interesting about God's *unfallen* creatures that highlights the fact of their purity, which is described as a *bright shining light*.

Did Adam and Eve have some type of light emanating from them acting as a protective covering, or simply as a covering, which was God's mark upon His creation? Certainly, if that was the case, then the fall would absolutely destroy that light covering. It destroyed a number of other things as well, and created other things.

It is very likely that the fall caused God to create *entropy*, which prior to the fall would not have existed. Entropy is what makes people old, causes sickness, and ultimately, ushers in death. Would that have existed before the fall? In a word, *no*, because God said that everything He had made was *good*.

But humanity has learned little. What Adam and Eve did then – trying to become like gods by leaving God out of the picture – is no different from what people do today.

The message from the fourth dimension is the same. We can be like gods. We will then live fourth dimensionally, always living divinely, never again succumbing to the faults of living only in the third dimension.

This is the plan that Satan has instructed his minions to teach unwary human beings. It is a plan that is as old as the ages, yet snares new people every day. The idea that ordinary people have divinity resident within them is something most want to have and experience. To be god and to be free of the habits that keep humanity in its unenviable downtrodden state is certainly a goal worthy of achieving. Why, though, is this goal predicated on *self-effort?* It is a way in which humanity can become gods without needing God's help. In fact, the antiquated idea of the God of the Bible is just that; antiquated and outmoded.

Modern human beings need to grow beyond that claustrophobic and severely limited understanding of God. The true god is beyond limits and cannot be contained in one book, even if it is the Bible. The true god is beyond description, except for the description of *love*. This is the only god that humanity needs. Any other god is either a false god or one that is not fully understood and therefore limited. This is what humanity is being taught by ascended masters, spirit guides, aliens, and the like.

To truly become free, each individual must grab hold of the goal that leads to the ideal of fourth dimensional divine living. That is the plan and the plan omits God. Can anything good come from something that deliberately omits God, the Creator of all things?

5

The "Light" that is Not

It really does not matter whether or not the *source* of the message is an *alien*, *ascended master*, or *spirit guide*. In fact, it is likely that the *source* is exactly the same, in spite of what the messenger wants us to believe. What matters most is the message itself that's being relayed to humanity.

In virtually all cases – aliens, ascended masters, spirit guides – all speak of greater understanding, which to them means more *light*, as in getting more light on the subject. The more light there is in the world, the greater the understanding. The greater the understanding, the more people there are who are connected with that understanding. Ultimately, those beings in the fourth dimension want humanity to comprehend one thing: *we control our destiny*. There is no personal God, as in the Bible. What many call gods were at one time what we are now.

This is the message and of course it is a dangerous one, as we have learned, because it pushes God out of the picture completely. He is replaced with human beings, who come to believe – as did Lucifer – that we are gods and need no other outside of ourselves.

This lie, told boldly to adherents of the occult, the New Age movement, and a host of esoteric groups and societies, is one that takes root quickly within each individual because it caters to our *pride*. The more *impersonal* this light can become for us, the greater the chances that people will be willing to explore it.

Impersonal forces do not make people feel guilty over what may be considered to be *sin*. In fact, there is little in the world that is said to be truly evil. People who do bad things are simply working out their karma. Like all of us, they have many new lives in front of them to work things out. They will eventually climb on board with the rest of humanity, or they will be removed.

Those who masquerade as aliens and other entities do so because they want to deceive human beings into thinking that we are *self-made*. Think about it. Even evolutionists are now considering the concept that the true beginnings of life that occurred on this planet were seeded here by superior intellects from other planets, galaxies, or dimensions. Even if this could by some freak chance be remotely true, it *still* does not mean that human beings are gods. The idea that people have the inherent ability to control forces *outside* of themselves in order to become creators themselves is absurd because it goes against logic, yet that is what more and more people are doing. How can something that is created ever be more than *created*?

How is it possible for the *created* to be the *creator*? I'm not simply talking about being able to invent something, or to create something using materials that already exist. I'm talking about creating out of nothing. No one would be able to invent something if resources did not already exist on this planet.

Creation is a process that only God can accomplish because He created from nothing (*ex nihilo;* literally *out of nothing*). What human beings do is to *put together* aspects of God's Creation like a puzzle in order to make what was not *seen* before. This does not mean the resources were not there before. It simply means that whatever a person is said to have created was done by taking various *pre-existing elements*, doing something to them, or combining them in such a way as to make something new. Yet without those pre-existing elements and resources, nothing new would have been "created."

God is the only One who created something out of nothing. This we understand from the first chapter of Genesis. That is what it means to be a true Creator. What human beings do is more akin to being an alchemist.

Science takes the time to study existing aspects of the Creation. From those studies, determinations are made. Some of those determinations can be cataloguing or combining.

Recently, I watched a documentary on how far body armor has come. What used to weigh a great deal because it was made of steel now weights far less than half that because good body armor is now made of porcelain covered in Kevlar. Who would have thought that the lighter weight porcelain would offer better protection than steel?

Did man create steel? Yes, by combining certain elements with fire. Did man create porcelain? Yes, by combining specific elements. Again, no one created the raw material that goes into the creation of either steel or porcelain. In that sense then, it cannot be accurately stated that man truly *creates*. At best, he comes up with a new way of combining elements to form something that has not been formed prior.

People are so quick to rule out the possibility of one, true, personal God because if He exists, that instantly means that people are responsible to Someone and must give an accounting of our lives. It makes sense that if God exists and He created, then naturally He would expect us to provide an accounting for how we lived in this life.

However, if we are *already* gods in some form, then the only one we answer to is *ourselves*. This is the thrust of the idea *behind* the message. It is to pull us further away from the God of the Bible so that we become more inward in our approach to life. This message is diametrically opposed to Scripture and it is diametrically opposed to Jesus, who spent His entire life submitting not to Himself, but to God the Father. Though God Himself, Jesus did this to show humanity *how* we are to live. He also did this to fulfill every aspect of the law in order that He would become an acceptable sacrifice for our sin.

Here is the dilemma. Ever since humanity failed the test and opted to follow their own desires *away* from God, we have continued along those lines, hoping to find some way of avoiding the guilt that is associated with the road that takes people away from God. No one likes to feel guilty and when we do, we do one of two things:

1. *Feel badly enough to confess it in the hopes of feeling relieved of the guilt, or*
2. *Dig in our heels because of our pride and refuse to acknowledge that something is wrong*

In essence, the lie that we are being told today is a lie that keeps us from returning to God. It makes us think that we are all we need and if we will just learn to listen to our own inherent divinity, then all will be well with the world.

This is the lie that keeps people from God! Because human beings feel guilty about things they have done, they tend to blame God for it, rather than simply admit that they messed up.

If you look closely at the Genesis account in chapter three, it is clear that Eve blamed the serpent and Adam blamed Eve *and* God! The serpent kept his mouth shut because he knew exactly what he had done and was actually quite happy about it. He felt he knew that this would so destroy God's plan for His Creation that he (the serpent) was now in control. Wrong.

People would rather blame someone else than accept blame for what they have done. Esoteric teachings reveal that if someone is murdered, they one murdered was somehow inviting it. This does not absolve the person who perpetrated the act of murder, but the higher level of thinking here is that *both* people are/were working out their karma. It is a fact of the way life goes.

Esoteric teachings *devalue* human life. If you stop to consider it, those who are deeply into the esoteric often have a greater degree of respect for animals and Mother Earth than people. It is because people are the ones who live by reason. That reason can essentially get us to the spiritual plane where we are fully in charge of our own life. Animals cannot do this and are therefore relegated to living on *instinct*. Because of this vast difference, human beings are seen more and more as *causing* problems for this world and for the animal kingdom. Following that to its natural end means that it is the responsibility of all human beings to ensure that animals are not used for man's selfish purposes (you know, like *eating*), but are instead cared for in order that they will survive for future generations.

Becoming more aware of the tenets and teachings of the esoteric reveals why there are so many liberal, bleeding hearts. These people are unable to see the world in any way except through the brainwashing that they have experienced. In it, the entire Creation is reversed in its order.

Genesis tells us that human beings are the pinnacle of God's creation because God breathed life into man and he became a living soul (cf. Genesis 1-2). He did not do that with animals or any other aspect of His Creation, including angels. Except for man, God created everything else without breathing into them in order that they might have life.

The esoteric inverts this concept so that man is really at the bottom of the poll, here to serve everything else while being a good custodian of all the resources on this planet. As a Christian, this does not mean that I can use and abuse what God has provided on this planet for my own self-centered means. However, it is clear from Scripture that eating meat is not a bad thing. It is clear also that having animals to provide for humanity is not in opposition to God's original plan.

Living creatures outside our dimension tell us that we must gain new understanding through the light that is available to us. We must train ourselves to see that light, and once seen, it must be embraced. The stated end goal is to become one with everything else in the universe. In doing so, the individuality of each person is not only degraded, but eventually evaporates.

God's true biblical plan places high value on people and on the individual. God wants us to succeed, but He wants us to succeed on His terms because He knows that His way is the only right way. Anything else is second best, and second best is never good enough.

6

Language of Aliens

One of the things that we find rampant throughout the messages that are transmitted by aliens, ascended masters, or spirit guides is the use of biblical language. This is part of the deception and it works.

Routinely, what these entities do is incorporate familiar-sounding phrases and names within their messages. They will speak of "Christ," except they will add "the" in front of it. What they are referring to is not a specific person – as in Jesus Christ – but merely an *office*, an office that can be held by anyone who is able to attain to that particular level.

By referring to "the Christ," of course, this fully devalues Jesus Christ, as if He is merely one of many. The deeper that a person gets into the esoteric, the more clear this becomes. It is important that at first, the entities keep things sounding "Christian."

Let's take a look at the previously quoted *Great Invocation* for a moment to see if this holds true.

> *From the point of Light within the Mind of God*
> *Let light stream forth into the minds of men.*
> *Let Light descend on Earth.*
>
> *From the point of Love within the Heart of God*
> *Let love stream forth into the hearts of men.*
> *May Christ return to Earth.*
>
> *From the centre where the Will of God is known*
> *Let purpose guide the little wills of men –*
> *The purpose which the Masters know and serve.*
>
> *From the centre which we call the race of men*
> *Let the Plan of Love and Light work out*
> *And may it seal the door where evil dwells.*
>
> *Let Light and Love and Power restore the Plan on Earth.*[8]

Glancing over the Great Invocation, one quickly realizes that there is a great deal of *Christian-sounding* verbiage. Let's remove the verbiage from the context:

- *Light*
- *Mind of God*
- *Love*
- *Heart of God*
- *Christ*

---
[8] http://www.lucistrust.org/en/service_activities/the_great_invocation__1

- *Will of God*
- *Evil*

Anyone who knows anything of the Bible and the teachings of Jesus has heard those words or phrases before. Jesus called Himself the Light of the world (cf. John 8:12). He essentially stated that the world was in darkness until His arrival. He brought light, because He *is* Light.

The apostle Paul speaks of being humble, as true followers of Jesus Christ. In his letter to the Philippians, Paul tells them that they should be as humble as Jesus. He says "*Let this mind be in you, which was also in Christ Jesus*" (Philippians 2:5).

Of course, the attribute most ascribed to the God of the Bible is *love*. We are all familiar with John 3:16, which tells us that God loved the world so much, He sent His son. Whoever believes on the work of Jesus shall be saved.

People wind up actually misappropriating the idea of love, falsely attributing to God the wrong idea of love. People wrongly believe that God is love to the exclusion of all else. In fact, with God, there is a perfect balance of holiness, justice, hatred (of sin), and much more.

God is not merely defined by love alone. That is a feature of His character, one that humanity will never be able to emulate. However, God is far more multi-faceted than human beings like to admit.

We have seen that so far, the language used in the Great Invocation is such that anyone who has had any upbringing in any church will be familiar with the terms used within Christendom. This alone will cause people to let their guards down when they come across something like this for the first time.

They will read through it and since they are familiar with much of the wording will not think that anything is wrong. How could it be wrong, they wonder, since the wording is so Christian-sounding?

This is what the enemy of our souls does. He entraps us with carefully laid schemes that remind us of something else, and what they remind us of is known to us. Since it is known to us, we feel comfortable with it and find no fault in it.

It would be foolhardy for these aliens and other entities to attempt to deceive humanity by tossing completely new ideas at us. That would cause red flags for certain in many.

However, if they take what humanity is already familiar with and then simply modify the meaning, they have something that too many will swallow because of the familiar air to it.

Jesus Christ is not a Person per se. The Christ is a *consciousness* or *position* that a person attains to and in so doing, begins to live divinely and fourth dimensionally.

This is the goal of Satan and his minions. He desires with all of his heart to deceive as many people as he can. To that end, he has created a very slippery slope for human beings, a slope that all too many human beings are willing to risk climbing.

7

Who Are They...Really?

It is probably best at this point to talk about the identities of those who spend their time channeling messages from other dimensions to human beings in this dimension. You have likely figured out by now that though I believe beings *do* exist in other dimensions, I do not trust them. In fact, if you have been paying attention, you know that I believe the immediate king over all of these entities and beings is none other than Satan himself.

If Satan is their Lord, then who are his underlings? We have two choices here. We can 1) read and believe what the Bible tells us, or

2) read and believe what the beings themselves tell us. That is a decision you must make for yourself, but my suggestion is that before you decide that the Bible needs to be cast off, think again.

Ask yourself what proof any of these beings have offered to show that they are who they say they are in their many ramblings and revelations. Can they prove beyond doubt to you that the Archangel Michael, for instance, *is* truly *the* Michael from Scripture?

It is one thing to talk the talk, but it is quite another thing to prove the talk. How many of you would simply open the door to an individual who is dressed like a police officer late at night without asking for some type of proof of identity? The problem, of course, is that logic tells you that they are wearing a police officer's uniform, therefore they must be a police officer.

How many times have you heard about men impersonating law enforcement officials, pulling women over and then raping them? How many times have we read about individuals who have dressed like armored carrier personnel for the purpose of overcoming the real guards and running off with the money?

The world of espionage and con artists is predicated upon the idea that people will believe what they *see* and *hear* if it is presented in a manner that is believable. In fact, if we consider how effective people work, we know that one of the things they are able to do is present themselves in a manner that others accept as *authoritative*. Even when a person may not know what they're talking about – and who among us has not been around at least one person like that – if they present their argument with enough authority, it is very likely to be accepted.

This is the problem with hearing things from beings in other dimensions. First of all, the Bible forbids that we should give heed to anything some spirit says who does not reside in our dimension. Deuteronomy 18:9-14 alone is very clear on this subject.

"When thou art come into the land which the LORD thy God giveth thee, thou shalt not learn to do after the abominations of those nations.

*"10 There shall not be found among you any one that maketh his son or his daughter to pass through the fire, or that useth divination, or **an observer of times, or an enchanter, or a witch**.*

*"11 **Or a charmer, or a consulter with familiar spirits, or a wizard, or a necromancer**.*

*"12 **For all that do these things are an abomination unto the LORD**: and because of these abominations the LORD thy God doth drive them out from before thee.*

"13 Thou shalt be perfect with the LORD thy God.

"14 For these nations, which thou shalt possess, hearkened unto observers of times, and unto diviners: but as for thee, the LORD thy God hath not suffered thee so to do." (emphasis added)

This is only *one* instance in Scripture where God has specifically forbidden consulting with spirits or entities from the other dimension. Why? Aside from the fact that doing so is an abomination to God, the reality is that by consulting spirits – call them spirit guides, familiar spirits, aliens, ascended masters, or whatever – we are looking to *them* as though they are God. Beyond this, it is more than likely that these spirit guides are nothing more than demons, masquerading as spirit guides...or aliens...or ascended masters...or other esoterics.

How do we know this? Apart from Scripture, it is impossible to know it. If Scripture is set aside, the only proof anyone has is what the entities themselves present to us. What is to say that they are being truthful? What is to say that they are being altruistic, as they say they are being? What is there that is offered as proof by any one of these spiritual beings that what they say is the truth?

The only thing that is offered is their *word*. While they can project images into people's minds and provide *experiences* to people, the experience alone is not proof of anything. In other words, if I have a very vivid dream, when I wake, I will realize it was merely a dream.

A person who claims to have a vivid experience of flying through the dimensions of space as they leave their bodies has no proof of that experience. It could easily be a trick of the mind perpetrated by some entity living in the next realm.

If we look through the Bible, it is clear that these beings exist outside this dimension. It is also clear that they have some control over aspects within this dimension. The book of Job explains to us that Satan has the ability to take life. He also has the power to take away a person's health (cf. Job 2).

The notes in the MacArthur Study Bible list all of what Job suffered and all were perpetrated by Satan:

- *Painful boils from head to toe (2:7, 13; 30:17)*
- *Severe itching/irritation (2:7,8)*
- *Great grief (2:13)*
- *Lost appetite (3:24; 6:6,7)*
- *Agonizing discomfort (3:24)*
- *Insomnia (7:4)*
- *Worm and dust infested flesh (7:5)*
- *Continual oozing of boils (7:5)*
- *Hallucinations (7:14)*
- *Decaying skin (13:28)*
- *Shriveled up (16:8; 17:7; 19:20)*
- *Severe halitosis (19:17)*

- *Teeth fell out (19:20)*
- *Relentless pain (30:30)*
- *Raging fever (30:30)*
- *Dramatic weight loss (33:21)*[9]

If Satan is capable of controlling (or causing) these types of things that affect a person, then who really knows what else he is capable of doing? At the beginning of the book of Job, Satan is allowed to test Job from *without*, not directly on his person. Because of this, Satan sends neighboring armies, fire from heaven, and a tornado to take away Job's herds and family.

Do we truly know the limits of Satan's ability? Obviously, he is kept in check by God, who is infinitely greater of course, but in his own right, Satan is obviously – for now – a fearsome foe. If Paul tells us that he has the ability to transform into an angel of light, then that coupled with his ability should help us get a small glimpse of his full potential.

If Satan hates us as he hates Jesus, then it is clear that he likely hates all of humanity. It was this hatred and jealousy that prompted him to originally strike at God's Creation by targeting Eve and Adam to rebel against God as he (Satan) had done. If he was jealous of Adam and Eve, then chances are good that this jealousy extends to all of humanity.

In essence then, it is very possible that God's Creation of Adam and Eve wound up usurping Satan's, who had been created to be the highest being below God. Once he rebelled and was cast out of heaven, the only place he had to go was this planet and the air that encircles it.

Seeing then that God had created an individual (Adam) who was now in charge of God's Creation, where Satan had once been in charge of

---

[9] MacArthur Study Bible, NASB (Thomas Nelson, 2006), 692

the heavenly hosts, absolutely *galled* Satan. From that moment on, he would work to destroy God's ordered Creation by starting at the top with the pinnacle of that Creation...*man*. If he was successful in causing man to fall, he would at least regain some of what he lost (though only temporarily until his judgment) by becoming the *prince of this world* (cf. John 14:30).

As far as Satan is concerned, human beings are subservient to him. He fully believes we *should* serve him and in order to make that happen, he must devise a way that ensnares and enslaves as many human beings as possible. Certainly, he's not going to be upfront about the way he does it, either, but will use as much subterfuge as possible to reach his goals of world domination.

Satan has been using the entire area of aliens to create that subterfuge. It has gained the distinction of sounding so scientific. Over the centuries, the idea that aliens exist has become more pronounced. It would appear that in 2011, the time is just about ripe for the final reveal. Hollywood has spent decades preparing the masses by creating a type of reality fiction from science fiction.

That together with the New Age movement, the Theosophical Society, and other esoteric groups has pushed knowledge, mysticism, and existentialism to the forefront of man's thinking.
Why do people seek the advice of tarot cards, psychics, mediums, channelers, and the like? It is because we normally want to know something about the future, don't we? We are not content to live in the *now*, so we want to see where our life is going or what we can do to bring our dreams into our reality.

Spirit guides and others do *not* have privy to the future, though they pretend they do. They only know things in generalities, such as the fact that Jesus will return one day. They also know that this world will come to an end one day. Beyond this they know that they will be cast into the Lake of Fire for all eternity. In essence, they know the

Bible – what it says, what it teaches – and they understand it remarkably well. Because of this, they can easily twist it to their predetermined meaning, deceiving people in the process.

The prophesies in Scripture are known to them. But for them to try to figure out what is going to happen when and where, educated guessing is required on their part. They are often in the dark, as we are in the dark. Of course, they are not above making it up as they go along either.

When people yearn to know the future, these entities are more than happy to tell people what they want to hear. Once they do, it is something that people will often try to bring about, whether consciously or subconsciously. If it doesn't happen as it was revealed to them, they will often blame it on themselves.

Isn't this the exact same situation when we listen to people who attempt to con us out of something? I've been had and maybe you have too.

While you're going through the process, sometimes there is a weird feeling you get that acts as a red flag. Something is telling you to move away and forget the whole thing, but you override that instinct. You push on ahead and after all is said and done you realize that you were *taken* for a bit of a ride. It happens all the time in society and to many people on a daily basis.

If human beings do this to one another, why should we believe that entities who reside in the fourth dimension would not be capable of the same thing? Someone will say, *"Well, look at what these entities are telling us about love and living divinely. Shouldn't that mean that they are being honest?"* No.

Why does the Bible teach us to *test* the spirits if they are not capable of lying to us? *"Beloved, believe not every spirit, but try the spirits whether they are of God: because many false prophets are gone out into the world. Hereby know ye the Spirit of God: Every spirit that confesseth that Jesus Christ is come in the flesh is of God: And every spirit that confesseth not that Jesus Christ is come in the flesh is not of God: and this is that spirit of antichrist, whereof ye have heard that it should come; and even now already is it in the world"* (1 John 4:1-3).

What the apostle John is saying is that spirits are very capable of *lying*. For fallen angels, their natural language – like Satan's, their overlord – is lying. They exist to deceive. We know from the example of Jesus' temptation in the wilderness that Satan crafted special meanings for the Scripture he used to test Jesus (cf. Matthew 4).

Paul tells us that Satan himself is *transformed* into an angel of light (cf. 2 Corinthians 11:14). This should clue us into the fact that both fallen angels and Satan tell lies and present themselves as something they are not for their own purposes and gain. They *want* to deceive. That is their ultimate goal.

If they want to deceive us, the question must be asked *why* they want to deceive us. What possible purpose could they have to attempt to pull the wool over people's eyes? Let's see if we can determine the answer to that question.

8

The Fallen

Who is this Jesus anyway? This question was asked by an avenging angel named Azazel in the NBC TV mini-series called *The Fallen*. Aaron Corbet – a character on the show, who recently turned 18 and discovered he was one of the *Nephilim* – told him that *"a lot of people believe that Jesus is God's Son."*

Azazel's response to this was hearty laugh. Aaron asked him if he was serious that he had not known about Jesus, to which Azazel responded that he had "been away for a while." In fact, Azazel had been chained to a rock for 5,000 years. He was now free after making a deal with the devil to help protect Aaron, who, as it turns out, is *The Redeemer*. The Redeemer was prophesied to come and redeem those angels who had fallen so that they could return to heaven, their first estate.

Azazel certainly would have known of Jesus since the Bible declares Him to be God the Son, the Creator of all things (cf. John 1, Colossians 1, etc.). In essence, Azazel – a created being, as Lucifer and all other entities apart from God were created – would have known of God, which consisted then (and consists now) of three individuals; God the Father, God the Son, and God the Holy Spirit. But let's not let biblical facts stand in the way of a science-fiction mini-series.

The mini-series is based on novels by Thomas E. Sniegoski. There is of course a good deal of biblical imagery here as well as indirect references to the *Book of Enoch*, an extra-biblical manuscript that some commentators believe to have been authentically written by *the* biblical Enoch and carried on the Ark with Noah. It is clear that both Peter and Jude knew of this book because both writers either quote from it or reference it in their epistles. It is also likely that Jesus was familiar with it.

The mini-series starts out with a voice-over explaining the premise. Satan rebels. Angels rebel with him. They all fall to earth. Once there, the fallen angels distance themselves from Satan, cohabit with human women and have children that have the bodies and abilities of angles, but with the souls of men.

The series unfolds with the realization that other angels are out to destroy all the fallen angels wherever they are found. Of course, Aaron, who turns out to be one of the Nephilim, is hunted as well when he turns 18 and clearly becomes one. Interesting how the good angels seem more evil than the Nephilim in the mini-series.

Tom Skerritt plays one of the fallen angels who tries to help Aaron understand his predetermined role, not only as a Nephilim, but also as The *Redeemer*. Of course Aaron rebels against this idea, but is slowly brought around to the fact that that is the truth about him.

Aside from all of the extra-biblical fantasy here, there are plenty of references to New Age teachings and ideals. When Tom Skerritt's character mentions "the Creator," Aaron says, "*God?*" Skerritt laughs and says that the name "God" is too small to describe the Creator. He then sings out that whether it's Allah, Shiva, or something else altogether, the Creator is all of these things.

The problem with this mini-series is that it attempts to be seen as biblical, but it is far from it. It wears biblical clothing so to speak, but that's as far as it goes. While some may argue that screenwriter Tim Huddleston was merely taking some liberties, it is clear from anyone who knows Scripture at all that there is hardly anything in the series that coincides with Scripture, except some of the names of entities and the general idea that some good angels fell, becoming evil ones.

The angels in the mini-series are obnoxious and even swear. They are sarcastic and denigrating toward the "creator." They fight to kill and make deals with the devil. Above all, the entire premise of the series is way off base. Scripture never indicates that the fallen angels, once having fallen, ever left Satan's loyalties. Beyond this, there is never any indication in Scripture that Nephilim are able to be redeemed. Once fallen, they remain fallen, unlike human beings who have the chance to be redeemed through God's plan of salvation.

The reason for this difference is due solely to the fact that only humanity was created in God's image (Genesis 1-2). God literally breathed into man and Adam became a living soul. This is not true of the angels or animals.

The Fallen essentially supports much of the New Age and their view of aliens. There are many references within the world of aliens to God (whatever God is said to be by these aliens) and our ability to become whatever we want to become. Though Aaron is one of the Nephilim in the series, it takes him time to realize he is someone other than what he has known all of his life. Once he learns his true identity, he begins the process of actualizing that true identity within him, drawing on all of the latent powers that stem from it.

This is no different than the metamorphosis that human beings are taught we will go through as we come to terms with our own inner *deity*. The process of unlocking that deity and living from that core or center is something that is to be achieved by all human beings.

The Fallen (like many movies before it) is really an operation manual to help humanity unlock our true potential. Once we do that, we acknowledge and embrace our deity, and from there will truly be able to make this world a far better place.

9

Preparing for War

Joseph Chambers (Prophecy Forum Newsletter) wrote an article titled *Satan is Practicing for Armageddon*. In it, he points out the fact that what we see occurring today is bound up within the New Age Movement. The problem is that like the TV series *The Fallen* and movies like *Knowing*, the biblical language and term-inology used within these vehicles (to unconsciously promote the New Age) can actually confuse many people.

In other words, Christian-sounding terminology is deceptive because there is usually another meaning applied to those terms that are often thought to be orthodox. I have pointed this out in this book and others I have written, and Chambers points this out as well. *"Biblical terminology literally fills the writings and language of the New Agers and occultic leaders. They talk about the number 666, about saving the world (not souls), and about a harmonious, peace-loving age when everybody lives happily ever after."*[10] He then quotes a number of individuals and sources that do that very thing.

"The blueprint for a peaceful, loving and harmonious world has been drawn. Prayer, meditation, positive affirmations, spiritual families and global healing events such as Live Aid and the World Peace Event all contribute to this blueprint." – Harmonic Convergence brochure

"Humanity is on the verge of something entirely new, a further evolutionary step unlike any other: the emergence of the first global civilization." – Thomas Berry, Catholic theologian

"I [see] images of a new heaven and a new earth…THIS WORLD will be saved. The planet will be healed and harmonized. We can let the kingdom come…which means that THIS WORLD can be transformed into a heaven right now…This is no fantasy. This is not scientific or religious fiction. This is the main event of our individual lives." – John Randolph Price, Organizer of the World Instant of Cooperation

"Every major religion of the world has similar ideals of love, the same goal of benefitting humanity through spiritual practice…The most important thing is to look at details of theology or metaphysics…I believe that all the major religions of the world can contribute to world peace and work together for the benefit of humanity if we put aside subtle metaphysical differences, which are really the internal business of each religion…The undying faith in religion clearly demonstrates the potency of religion as such. This spiritual energy and power can be purposefully used to bring about the spiritual conditions necessary for world peace." – Dalai Lama

---

[10] Joseph Chambers *Satan is Practicing for Armageddon*, www.pawcreek.org

"All human institutions, professions, programs and activities must be judged primarily according to the extent they either obstruct and ignore or foster a mutually enhancing human-earth relationship. That is how good and evil will be judged in the coming years." – Donald Keys

There are a number of problems with the thoughts of those quoted above. In short, they are directly opposed to the clear teaching of Scripture. Regarding the quote from the *Harmonic Convergence* brochure, this merely reveals that these individuals believe that to attain the level of living divinely in the fourth dimension, a world filled with goodwill and good works *must* become the norm for all people on the planet. For these people, goodwill (as evidenced by good works) will save individuals and ultimately the planet. However, the Bible tells us that we are *not* saved by works at all, but by the free gift of salvation made possible by Jesus (cf. Ephesians 2:8-10). Good works *stem* from authentic salvation, but not the other way around.

The third quote (from John Randolph Price) again mixes truth with error. Yes, there will be a new heaven and a new earth, but it will only come *after* this one is destroyed by God (cf. Isaiah 65:17; Revelation 21:1-8). While Price may "see" images of a new heaven and earth, it will not be this one that becomes new, but new ones to fully replace the current ones.

Of course, people may ask, why should we listen to the Bible and not give heed to what these quoted individuals are saying, even if they *do* disagree with the Bible? Plainly, that is a decision that each person will need to make. It is based on the veracity of Scripture, over against the veracity (or not) of the individuals making their statements. It seems to me to be a simple decision to make.

The Bible – in my view – has certainly stood the test of time. Jesus fulfilled over 300 prophecies through His birth, life, death, and resurrection, with the first one generally acknowledged as Genesis

3:15. Jesus will fulfill many more as time moves toward the future reappearance of our Lord. What prophecies have Donald Keys, John Randolph Price, Thomas Berry, Dalai Lama, or any other individual spoken into fulfillment? None of which I am aware.

There are things occurring in this world as you read this that are creating the perfect situation for Satan's final assault on God's children and on God Himself. One of the ways he is bringing that about is through the preparation of those who follow his tune. They don't necessarily have to be occultists or worshippers of Satan. They can be atheists, agnostics, and seemingly moral or good people who hold to no particular religious ideology.

These people who have not sided with God of the Bible essentially stand against Him, whether they think so or not. There are only two plans for this earth: God's and Satan's. The question for each individual to answer is, which side do they choose? With whom will they stand? If not God, then it is Satan by default.

Consider the fact that during Jesus' days on this earth, Satan was not idle or dormant and neither were his spiritual minions. It was Satan himself who approached Jesus once He had been led by the Holy Spirit into the wilderness (cf. Matthew 4) for the express purpose of being tested by Satan.

Satan would not leave this extremely important test up to anyone other than himself. If anyone was going to bring Jesus down through temptation, it would be Satan. If successful, he would have watched the God-Man fall in defeat and this world would have been his forever. God's promises would then never come true.

However, it was not Jesus who failed, but Satan who failed, and he did so *miserably* as he routinely does. This did not stop him because he continued to assault God the Son without mercy then and God's authentic children since then. Yet, in all of these things, never once did Jesus stumble and sin. The Bible testifies to this fact in Hebrews 4:15. *"For we have not an high priest which cannot be touched with the feeling of our infirmities; but was in all points tempted like as we are, yet without sin."* While Jesus the Man was tempted as we are, He remained sinless. In Corinthians, Paul tells us *"For [God] hath made him to be sin for us, who knew no sin; that we might be made the righteousness of God in him"* (2 Corinthians 5:21). God made "Him" (referring to Jesus here) to be *seen* as sin, though Jesus Himself *never* sinned! He was absolutely impeccable in all things.

In Romans 8:3-4, Paul states that Jesus came into this world *in likeness* of sinful flesh. In other words, Paul was simply saying that from outward appearances, Jesus was every bit human as we are, but that is where the commonalities ended. Though he came into this world in *likeness* of human flesh (meaning, He *was* actually human, as opposed to those who said during Paul's time that Jesus was merely a *phantom*), he never once participated in sin at all. Again, the second letter to the Corinthians, chapter five, verse twenty-one gives testimony to the sinless state of Jesus. *"For he hath made him to be sin for us,* **who knew no sin***; that we might be made the righteousness of God in him."* (emphasis added)

The Bible is remarkably clear about the fact that Jesus never sinned. Peter also mentions this in 1 Peter 2:22, where he states, *"Who did no sin, neither was guile found in his mouth."* We know from the context here that Peter is referring to Jesus.

Since the Bible is clear that Jesus never sinned, we know that it was that fact that allowed Him to offer Himself as a sacrifice for *our* sins. This is a very personal thing, because it affects each individual. Once we recognize and agree with God that we *have* sinned and because of that we are literally strangers with God (He cannot have fellowship with us), it should bring us to the next level of realization, which is that God has provided a remedy for our sin. That remedy is found in Jesus' death on Calvary's cross and resurrection three days later. His shed blood secures our freedom *if* we submit to Him. We do this by acknowledging with our heart that Jesus is Lord (God) and that He died for the remission of sin, and then we verbally acknowledge that. Far from this being easy-believism, it is the way in which salvation is granted to the individual.

The New Age movement in no way agrees with that statement. To the New Ager, the world's "salvation" is bound up in *everyone* as a group. It is only as more and more people come to realize that this world must evolve to the next level that the group of people on this planet who desire "salvation" for this world, that the world has any chance of being "saved" from destruction.

Do you see the difference? New Agers tell us to enter into a higher state of "consciousness." They emphasize a "paradigm shift" so that we begin to think in global terms. No longer should we use resources of this earth if it means that future generations will go without. We can only reach the next spiritual plane through major and global acts of goodwill toward all people. It will be this that ushers in the "salvation" that this world awaits.

This sounds tremendous to millions of people throughout the world because there is nothing there that says everyone's *morals* must be the same. All each person needs to do is what Joseph Chambers relates that the New Age teaches, and that is to "*change our thought patterns to peace, harmony, and goodwill to everybody (except those religious maniacs called Jesus followers) [and] we can evolve to the next round on the evolutionary scale...*"[11]

I fully agree with Chambers when he calls this "*nothing but Satanic delusion.*"[12] But this sounds so good to people because of the absence of a specific set of moral standards. People are allowed to live their lives as they see fit *while* they take the time to visualize world peace.

---

[11] Joseph Chambers *Satan is Practicing for Armageddon*, www.pawcreek.org
[12] Ibid

The New Age ideology puts no ethical constraints on anyone. Each person is free to live as they choose, only they must join together to bring in what we are told is missing from this world.

The New Age movement began and has been growing strongly since its inception, and that beginning goes all the way back to the Tower of Babel and a man named Nimrod (Genesis 11; in essence all the way back to the Garden of Eden). More and more people seem to be hearing and agreeing with the gobbledy-gook that is merely the same lie originally told to Eve and Adam. The serpent tempted them with thoughts of becoming gods. They took the bait, just as millions are doing today.

What is most interesting is that due to our fallen nature, we tend to think that we must actually work for something for it to be valid, at least in the area of religion. While throughout the world today there are millions of people who firmly believe that governments owe them something and they have no problem putting their hand out, palms up, these same people believe that salvation is given to those who *earn* it, to those who participate in the mantra that is spreading throughout the world. Go figure. It is the mantra that says that we all need to become one in purpose, spirit, and intent.

The more people Satan gets to and converts to his way of thinking, the greater and quicker he will be able to permeate society, turning it globally to his will. The goal is to completely take over society and he is on his way to doing just that, with God's permission.

The one main problem that continues to curtail this plan is the invisible Church, Christ's Bride. The Holy Spirit working in and through millions of believers throughout the globe is a tremendous blockade for Satan, keeping him from reaching his short-term goals. Those short-term goals will pave the way for his overreaching goal, which is world domination. Satan is limited by the presence of God's Holy Spirit in and through His Church.

As authentic Christians live their lives for God's glory, Satan is thwarted and limited. However, there *will* come a time when God's presence will briefly stand aside, allowing Satan nearly free reign on this planet, something he has longed for since time immemorial in order to really stretch his wings.

As he prepares for the coming days before Armageddon, known as the Tribulation, it is clear that he is calling in all of his marks and everything that belongs to him. He is gaining their attention and lining them up for the final battle. It will be at least another seven years before that battle occurs, and to Satan's chagrin, it will be over before it starts (cf. 2 Thessalonians 2).

Just as Joseph Chambers says, Satan is *practicing* for Armageddon. He has a great deal to lose if he fails to gain the victory over Jesus upon His return. The Bible is clear that Satan *will* lose, but God's truth has never dissuaded him before and it won't then either.

10

Who is Satan?

Satan became without doubt the most narcissistic being that was ever created. He seems to forget that he was indeed actually *created*. He did not create himself, but was created by God, who gave Satan (Lucifer before his fall) the highest rank in heaven, under God alone.

When Satan fell, he battled it out with Michael and the rest of the angels. Satan lost and took one-third of the angels with him in his fall to earth. Unlike the TV mini-series *The Fallen*, the angels who fell with Satan did not desert him. Also unlike the mini-series, there is no redeemer who will come to redeem fallen angels, for the reasons already provided.

Because Satan never sleeps, he has worked tirelessly to get at least one step ahead of God and stay there. He has *never* managed to do that, though it is clear from Scripture that at times, he thought he was way ahead of God.

In the Genesis chapter 6 account of the time after the fall, we read of Nephilim. These beings are believed by many to be the result of some type of physical union between fallen angels and human women. The resultant Nephilim were essentially half-breeds, yet still fallen, just as their father was and remains.

The Nephilim, like everything else that was not on the Ark with Noah, died in the flood; at least their physical bodies died. However, their souls remained alive and lived to infest and infect other beings since that time. It is believed that these Nephilim became the demons of the New Testament that Jesus, Peter, Paul, and others dealt with in what has become known as exorcisms, when they (through the power of God) cast out these entities from everyday people.

We continue to see this phenomenon today and since these demons still exist, then it is clear that they still strongly desire a body to live in and at least have some control over. The last body that actually belonged to them was the one they were born with and inhabited prior to the Great Flood. Since that time, they have longed to regain what they lost.

The Book of Enoch tells the story of the original group of angels that God sent to earth to watch over man and God's Creation. Their job was essentially to protect man. Instead, they began lusting after women and found a way to cohabit with them. This would have been long *after* the fall of Adam and Eve. In fact, it was obviously during the time of Enoch (the seventh from Adam according to the geneology of Genesis 5 and Jude 1). God sent the angels to earth to protect humans from the onslaught of Satan and his minions. Instead, these "Watchers" (as they are called in the Book of Enoch) found some way to procreate with women and the women gave birth to what became known as the *Nephilim*, a hybrid creature of possible gigantic proportions and strength.

As mentioned earlier in this book, both Peter and Jude quote or refer to the Book of Enoch and they refer to this particular event, which caused God to chain these angelic beings so that they could no longer do what they did. They continue to remain in chains until their day of judgment. *"And the angels which kept not their first estate, but left their own habitation, he hath reserved in everlasting chains under darkness unto the judgment of the great day"* (Jude 1:6).

And again, in Jude 1:14-16, *"Enoch, the seventh from Adam, prophesied about them: "See, the Lord is coming with thousands upon thousands of his holy ones to judge everyone, and to convict all of them of all the ungodly acts they have committed in their ungodliness, and of all the defiant words ungodly sinners have spoken against him." These people are grumblers and faultfinders; they follow their own evil desires; they boast about themselves and flatter others for their own advantage."*

These passages reference the fact that angels left their first estate. Of course, commentators and scholars disagree over the actual meaning. Does it mean that the angels simply left heaven and fell to the earth, or does it mean that the angels who were given a specific command to be on the earth, watch over and protect humanity actually wound up going way beyond their angelic bounds by lusting after and finding a way to mate with human women? Was it the fact that the angels fell through sin, or was it the fact that they somehow found a way to cohabit with human beings, or was it *both*?

The fact that Genesis 6 tells us about the Nephilim and the giants that resulted from the union of "sons of God" with "daughters of men" seems to indicate that angels (*sons of God*, as also used in the book of Job) found a way to procreate with women, and the result was the

Nephilim half-breed offspring that had so changed God's natural creative order into something monstrous that God was forced to banish these angels to darkness in chains until their day of judgment.

Peter mentions this in his second letter. *"...God spared not the angels that sinned, but cast them down to hell, and delivered them into chains of darkness, to be reserved unto judgment"* (2 Peter 2:4). These are the same angels that Jude refers to here. They did something so terrible that God banished them and confined them to chains until their day of judgment.

God created everything and each animal or human procreated after their own kind (cf. Genesis 1-2) and everything was *good*. Some angels came along and threw a huge monkey works into things by going after beings that were not of their kind. The resultant offspring was neither fully angelic or fully human. It was a cross between the two and it was something that God would not say was *good*.

Satan is the most evil of all beings. If we consider the things that he has prompted people throughout this world to do, we see that evil on display from the beginning. He was the first murderer (cf. John 8:44), causing Cain to murder Abel. Satan has worked to created chaos, envy, jealousy, pride – all the things that are found in him and the very things that brought about his fall.

Satan works tirelessly to bring the final man of sin (cf. 2 Thessalonians 2) to the forefront of humankind's preordained destiny. He will find a way to completely indwell this individual and possibly even incarnate him so that the thoughts and ideals of Satan will be firmly embedded and enmeshed within the man of sin. Just as the Christians' destiny is to become more like Christ in character, so will the man of sin be so like his father that the two will be indistinguishable for all intents and purposes.

Satan's goal from the beginning has been to overthrow God. He has wanted to make God obselete, replacing God with himself, a created being that is *finite*, whereas God is *infinite*.

The ridiculousness of the equation is something that most can see, yet Satan barrels onward seemingly oblivious to the asinine nature of his own quest. The most tragic part of the entire thing is that he has managed to trap and indoctrinate so many into his web of lies and deceit. They are fully unable to see that they are caught up in his deceptions and consider themselves to be free thinking individuals who use their freedom to remain free. Unfortunately, as will inevitably be shown to them, their freedom is only imaginary.

Satan wants one thing and one thing only – to become God – but the very idea that someone can become something they are not is absurd to human beings, at least on the face of it. If a person is not, for instance, born of "royal blood," they cannot all of a sudden become royalty without marrying into it. In that case, they have become royal not because of themselves, but only because of the individual with whom they are connected. Without that connection, they cease to have any semblance of royalty. They themselves are still not royalty, but are merely *treated* as such due to the other person.

In essence, this is the way it is for authentic Christians. We became brothers and sisters of Jesus Christ through His redemptive mission when He came to this earth the first time. It is through our union with Him, through faith, that we are then *seen* as God's sons and daughters. Remove Jesus from the picture and we remain fallen human beings, incapable of saving ourselves from anything.

This is the lie that Satan tells his followers. *"Stick with me and you will become gods!"* Against all logic, people believe and adopt this attitude, clinging to one who is as finite as they. A finite human being associated with a finite fallen angel still equals being finite. Only in being connected to the infinite God of the universe and beyond does finite become eternal, and that is only done through faith in the life, death, and resurrection of Jesus Christ (cf. Romans 10:11-13).

Satan is on a path of complete, utter, and eternal destruction. That path will never change, regardless of what he says to those who place their trust in him. Satan's appointed future lies in the Lake of Fire, for all eternity. Those who follow him, believing that they will somehow receive a greater and better reward than their god (Satan), will come to realize that they have been the victim of the greatest con every perpetrated on humanity! Are you one of them? I pray not.

Regarding the Nephilim, as stated, though the original bodies of the Nephilim died in the flood, they remain with us. These, together with the fallen angels and Satan himself, are doing their best to guide this world toward Satan's intended agenda. He desperately wants to fulfill his goals.

The most obvious place that this is coming together is in the area of religion. Ray Gano of Prophezine.com states, "*In the last days we know that a one world religion will rise as a mighty phoenix. We see that taking place right before our eyes, and yet, no one is aware of it rising.*"[13] Gano then points out the connection between Roman Catholicism, New Age, and Humanism. This is why, he says, it is difficult to see the entire picture, because there are many components to Satan's plan.

We have attempted to bring all these various components together in this one book and it is nearly impossible to do. What caters to one person may be lost on another. Satan knows this of course and is quite content to provide the opening that caters to each person. If they are not Catholic, for instance, then maybe the New Age movement will be able to suck them in. If they are not into either of

---

[13] Ray Gano, *My Name is Lucifer*, prophezine.com

those, then maybe there is something within the field of humanism that will tempt their spirit.

For those who believe that neither New Age thought nor humanism is something that they think about or are moved by, there are plenty of other avenues. Death Metal or Black Metal music is one that has really tapped the minds of youth today. In fact, much of it (as we have discussed in previous books) is wholly satanic, leaving nothing to the imagination. Many of these songs are literally *prayers* and odes to Satan put to music (if you can call that music).

Gano rightly points out that focusing on individual aspects of what Satan is attempting to accomplish causes us to miss the "mother of all harlots" (cf. Revelation 17:5). This harlot is a conglomeration of all that is opposed to God in any form. The result is what the Bible calls the mother of all harlots because it is able to encapsulate a *something for everyone* mentality.

The harlot spoken of here in Revelation 17 is essentially a "mystery." Verse five in Revelation 17 states:

"And upon her forehead was a name written,

MYSTERY,

BABYLON THE GREAT,

THE MOTHER OF HARLOTS AND ABOMINATIONS OF THE EARTH."

Gano asks the question, *what is the mother of all false religions?* He tells us the answer is *Baal worship*. If we search the Scriptures, we will see just how old Baal worship is and how badly it affected (or even *infected*) the lives of the Israelites. Consider just one event in Scripture that tells of Elijah's contest with the prophets of Baal (cf. 1 Kings 18). That event in Elijah's life represents a cataclysmic situation that occurred between the god of this world and the true

God of the Universe. It is interesting to note that according to the text, the god of this world did not let out a "peep" even after the prophets of Baal yelled for his attention and cut themselves in the hopes that shedding their blood would cause him to respond. He didn't. Yet when it was Elijah's turn, God spoke mightily! Please read that text. Satan was silenced.

What is further fascinating about Gano's study here is that he takes the reader back to the original Hebrew in Isaiah 14 and unmasks Satan's name from the text! It turns out that Heylel Ben Shachar is Hebrew for the English transliteration of Lucifer. Further breaking this down, Gano points out that the name Heylel Ben Shachar literally means *Crescent moon/morning star*.[14] The final nail in the coffin, so to speak, is seen in Gano's revelation that "*The crescent moon and the*

---

[14] Ray Gano, *My Name is Lucifer*, prophezine.com

morning star is the symbol of Baal, the original false religion of Babylon, the mother of harlots."[15]

It is easy to determine that there are many companies today that use the symbol of the crescent moon/morning star in their logos. In a sense, then, Satan's name is hiding in plain sight all around us and most are not even aware of that fact! A very small sampling is shown on the chart on the previous page. From the Nuclear Security Summit to the Missile Defense Agency to Obama Youth and others, the crescent moon and star is clearly seen.

The Shriners' and Masonic logos date back to the time of ancient Babylon. The Masonic logo is replete with symbols dedicated to Satan. The "G" stands for God, but not the God of the Bible. Note also that the compass and square form the shape of the triangle, something we noted earlier that is important to the New Age movement.

I would wholeheartedly agree with Gano when he notes that *"Satan is one who likes symbols. We know this for a fact because in the end he will make all take his name in their right hand or forehead as stated in Rev 13:16-18, which tells us about the mark of the beast."*[16]

Satan fell due to his extreme *narcissism*. He continues doing what he's doing in the world because of that same narcissism. It was his narcissism that caused his fall and it will be his narcissism that will be his ultimate undoing. The natural result of his ego will grant him an eternity without God, all because he thought that he was someone who could overthrow God. Not only will he *not* overthrow God, but during that upcoming eternity without God, Satan will experience (like everyone else in the Lake of Fire) an eternity of God's *wrath*. That wrath will never be quenched because those in the Lake of Fire will never stop sinning.

---

[15] Ibid
[16] Ray Gano, *My Name is Lucifer*, prophezine.com

One of the most important aspects of Satan that we should understand about him is his superior intelligence. We are not comparing his intelligence to God's, but to *man's*. Satan is the highest created being and his intelligence is so far superior to the smartest human being that there really is no comparison. It is because of this intelligence that his deceptions are so difficult for those who are unaware to spot.

I was cruising the 'Net looking for symbols that utilized the crescent moon and stars and came across a Web site that poked fun of "right wingers" (including Christians apparently) and noted that right wingers fear the crescent moon and stars. On the contrary, I certainly do not *fear* it. I recognize it for what it is; one of the symbols that Satan has used to permeate the world so that at every turn, there is some type of reminder of him. He has literally hidden himself in plain sight and very few notice it, yet the subconscious mind notices it.

Because of this and his intelligence, he is probably the most dangerous when he is revealing himself as an "angel of light," as Paul speaks about in his letter to the Corinthians. In the eleventh chapter of second Corinthians, Paul takes the time to fight the claim that he is not truly an authentic apostle, but is simply taking advantage of the Corinthians, as some charged.

Paul is obviously frustrated, and who wouldn't be? In the beginning of the chapter, he is even slightly sarcastic, asking, *"Would to God ye could bear with me a little in my folly: and indeed bear with me"* (v. 1). He continues in an effort to point out what should be obvious to the believers at the church at Corinth. Finally, he charges that the people who are filling their minds with doubt about him are false prophets and they ultimately mean to shipwreck their faith.

After concluding this, Paul without equivocation states, *"For such are false apostles, deceitful workers, transforming themselves into the apostles of Christ. And no marvel; for Satan himself is transformed into an angel of light"* (2 Corinthians 11:13-14). He follows this up by applying that fact to the situation that then existed by telling the Corinthians that the men who were causing trouble were doing nothing more than *pretending* to be ministers of righteousness (cf. v. 15), yet they were filled with deceit, making them false apostles.

The fact that Satan not only transforms *himself* into an angel of light, but helps his own ministers (fallen spirit beings *and* human beings) appear to be righteous is a small feat for him, but creates tremendous problems within the visible Church. These situations should be noted and the people creating the problem should be dealt with according to the guidelines laid out in Scripture.

This type of situation occurs in churches all the time because of the fact that not all people who attend church are *authentic* Christians. Even those who are authentic can and do give into their sin nature and act from their fallen humanness instead of depending upon God for His strength and discernment.

If these things can occur in churches, how much greater and easier is it to see these things happen *outside* of the visible Church, in the world itself? The people in the world use their own feelings and moral code to determine what is right and what is wrong. These individuals have nothing to fall back on except themselves. They generally believe that if they are not hurting anyone, then they can't be wrong. They wind up becoming their highest authority, but tragically, they will answer to One who is infinitely higher.

The New Age movement takes it a few steps further. They believe and teach that even when someone is murdered or experiences some other tragedy it is likely due to their *karma* attracting it because there was something in their life that needed to be worked out. Don't forget that many within the New Age believe in some form of reincarnation. Each person has many lifetimes to correct problems and overcome areas in their life that need correction and overcoming. While the concepts of the New Age sound easy, admittedly, they are difficult to put into effect on a daily basis. In fact, attempting to work through the process taught within the New Age to activate a person's inherent deity is far more difficult than the average person cares to acknowledge. It takes a good amount of time and meditative effort and that is part of the draw. Because people have to work so hard at it, it becomes that much more compelling and inviting for people. They feel that they are onto something, so they continue, trying to achieve what other "enlightened" individuals have achieved; individuals like Jesus.

This works together to bring humanity to the point of being able to usher in a new spiritual existence on this earth. It comes about through a global consciousness and it is led by none other than Satan himself, who remains in shadows.

While most people laugh at the idea that Satan exists, he is the one who laughs the hardest because he continues to litter his name, his ideas, and his presence *throughout* society, unabated. He has done everything except appear visibly and announce that he exists (and who would believe him even then, except diehard Satanists)! Though he remains cloaked in invisibility, his narcissism won't allow him to remain there completely. He *must* do things that will cause people to know he exists, either consciously or unconsciously.

Because of his tremendous ego, he works tirelessly toward the day when he will rule the world and dethrone God. While he *will* rule for a short period of time, he will never succeed in removing God from His rightful throne.

11

The Forces That Shape Us

As time has progressed since Madame Blavatsky and Alice A. Bailey introduced their esoteric writings to the world, a good deal has changed. Decades ago when these two women lived, the ideas propagated through their writings was read and embraced by a far smaller group than exists today. Today, millions and millions of individuals have little problem adopting aspects of their writings.

In fact, it has become so popular today that to talk of Alice A. Bailey as an occultist does not even raise an eyebrow for most people. What was certainly shocking generations ago is common today.

In our last chapter, we talked about Satan, a bit of his origins, and his overall demeanor and attitude. We talked about the fact that he has literally permeated society with his name and at this point in time he does not really care that for many, awareness of him may be relegated to the subconscious. He knows that there will be a time when all will worship him and they will do so through his incarnate son, the Antichrist, even though it will be extremely short-lived.

But Satan has also worked very hard to *desensitize* society to his thoughts, teachings, and ideas through many venues. Of course his teachings and ideas first came to the fore in modern times through Blavatsky and Bailey. In those days, things were discussed behind closed doors for fear of reprisals. No one wanted to have to deal with being called a witch then. Better to remain sequestered behind closed doors so that people would not really know what went on there unless they were believers themselves.

Because of the severe strain of egomania that is part of Satan's make-up, there is no way that he would allow that to remain as it was, so ways to incorporate his teachings throughout society would need to be determined. We have talked about some of these things before, but it is important and necessary to present them here as well. We are going to finish this book by discussing a number of areas in which Satan's ideologies have become the norm for much of society. How has that happened? Many would not openly attend a Satanic mass. No, in order for Satan to broadcast his particular perspective, it would have to be done subconsciously, in terms that *seemed* to be fairly innocuous to the average person.

If that same average person got wind of the idea that they were in fact worshipping Satan, most would run and close the door tightly behind them. In light of that, Satan carefully considered a plan to bring his ideas to fruition so that it would simply one day appear that they had always been part of society. This has been done through a number of venues that we will consider:

1. New Age movement
    a. Including books and workshops
2. Hollywood
    a. Including TV and movies
3. The Record Industry
4. The News Media
    a. Including the Internet
5. Aliens

As will be seen, a number of these areas overlap and in some sense it is difficult to know when one ends and another begins. Regardless, it is important to note that Satan has successfully impacted the whole of society by simply taking control of the above areas. People have literally been brainwashed over time because of the constant repetition of Satan's "party" line in which his lies and filth are broadcast openly.

Think about the fact that twenty or thirty years ago, pornography was pretty much in the closet. If someone wanted pornography, they had to go to some store where they could watch "peep" shows in a private booth. It was also rare to see more than a breast or two in many movies. Full frontal nudity was not shown unless the movie was an "X-rated" movie. R-rated movies did not show a great deal.

Over time, it became more acceptable to show more, including simulated coitus. The reason for this is simple. The Internet created the opportunity for people to watch porn in the privacy of their own homes and they did not have to go sneaking out to a porn store. The other reason porn took off and slowly became more mainstream is simply due to the fact that people got tired of the same thing. It became boring so they pushed the envelope a bit, to the next level.

This is exactly the way drugs work. Studies have shown that many addicts have been created from the recreational use of marijuana. The same activity over time can become stale, so people want to increase the level of excitement. To do this, a more powerful drug needs to be ingested or the body won't recognize the difference.

Think about food. Your favorite food may be pizza, from your favorite pizza place. Try eating that pizza every day for a while and it will not be too long before your taste buds are demanding a break from it. They want something else.

This is the way humanity is and it is largely due to our fallen nature. We become tired of the same old thing, so we want to push it up a notch.

At the same time, there have been elements in society who have helped by condemning those who complain about pornography. We are told that if we don't like it, don't look at it (as if we spend our time looking at it). We know the dangers of pornography on the mind of the average person, yet instead of recognizing that, people scream "freedom of expression!"

The entertainment industry has played a huge part in changing the way society sees things like sexual mores. When I was in high school, yes, girls wore mini-skirts, but if you compare that with the way people dress today, there are many cases where there is not even a modicum of decency. It is as if anything goes.

Look at the way people *talk* these days. The F-bomb is normal. Attitudes of respect are severely lacking. We have seen a tremendous change in the way people act and speak in our society today. Movies and television have brought this about. Hollywood has always argued that they have simply *reflected* the values of society. This is simply not true. They have been on the forefront of *changing* those values to make it much more acceptable for them to push the envelope. Ultimately, they wish to create a society which reflects the values (or lack of them) of Hollywood.

Hollywood wants to destroy any sense of Christian values and mores, replacing them with *relative* values, values that can and do change depending upon the situation. Christian values are absolute and fewer and fewer people want to deal with those. Give them relative values and relative truth every time because that allows them to respond to a given situation in the way they see fit, not the way that God tells them they should respond.

The movie industry has been leading the charge to eradicate and replace Christian values with values that are susceptible to the changing outlook in society. It amazes me how movies have changed over the past few decades.

When I watch a show from when I was a kid, the difference in that and today's shows is *stark*. Today's shows are far grittier, unquestionably sexual with a moving palate of ethics. Most often, the dad is a moron and his kids know infinitely more than he does, as does his wife. They put up with dad because he's dad and in some sense they actually feel sorry for him.

I recall when the TV animated show *Family Guy* started. It seemed okay to watch. However, it was not long before just about everything in the show became laced with sexual innuendo. In fact, much of it was not even innuendo but outright statement.

This has happened with any number of shows that start off relatively fine, but quickly turn into something that seems to have clawed its way out of the pit of hell. This is what people watch and *enjoy* today. It is part of their normal, daily lifestyle.

Movies and television shows have a sneaky way of forcing their views on people. They do not do this by having someone sit in a chair and talk *at* the viewer. People would reject that out of hand if they did not agree with the position of the speaker (besides which it would be extremely boring). Movies and television shows consistently present opinions, attitudes, and demeanors as *normal* within given situations around which the main actors engage. There is always a way in which things that have long been on the outskirts of society find a way into the more routine areas of that society.

This is most obvious with the Gay and Lesbian watchdog groups. Over the past several decades, gays and lesbians have been portrayed as individuals with lifestyles that simply need to be accepted for who they are as people. There is nothing wrong with accepting people as people, but the problem is that many of these same TV shows and movies portray the religious person as the *persecutor* of the gay individual.

The stereotypical religious legalist is one of the favored antagonists of today. They are easy to hate. These shows will then have a *liberal* religious person who enters with a "live and let live" or "love all people" approach to show that it is the *liberal* religious person who really understands what love is all about. The legalist should be shunned. What is missing is the way Jesus would have approached the issue. He would have offered salvation and then said, "*Go and sin no more.*" This position does not play well on TV or in movies, since it is difficult to agree with that position. Moreover, the concept of "sin" is not something that most want to hear about or entertain thoughts of.

The basic formula in most movies and TV shows is to set up the problem with an antagonist, normally coming against someone that the audience can see as the *underdog*. Once the show has set the parameters, the audience naturally follows along as if they are watching *real life* happen right in front of them. Of course, they are simply watching a script unfold, but that makes no difference to the audience. The people in the audience *invest* their emotions into the scenes and it is from those *emotions* that they make their decisions.

The better the script and actors, the better the emotional response from the viewer. Once this is replicated times 1,000 over the course of several years, what began as a seed planted in the mind has grown into a solid oak tree. People no longer ask *why* they believe something. They simply *believe* it because it *feels* right. Their rationale is based on how they have grown to feel about something and that stems from the quality of the presentation they have witnessed repeatedly.

I recall Jim and Tammy Faye Bakker's son Jay, who not long ago said that God *revealed* to him that homosexuality was *not* wrong. It goes without saying that the way in which God apparently revealed this to Jay was *extra-biblically* through the realm of emotions. In other words, it was not through Jay's study of Scripture that he came to this new understanding, but through his subjective *feelings*. It is now his passion to stand up for gays and lesbians. Where did he get that idea? Most likely from his mother, who was friends with many gays, especially after the entire debacle occurred when the PTL Club and ministries were taken from the Bakkers and Jim went to jail for his sexual proclivities. You reap what you sow and Jay is the result of his parents' thinking and teaching.

So when something like Prop 8 comes along in California, anyone who is in favor of Prop 8 (marriage is between one man and one woman) is seen as a *hater*. This is said enough times to make it "true," though of course it is not true. What is true is that the Bible proclaims that God is opposed to sin. Homosexuality is sin and like any sin, it (the *sin*, not the *person*) needs to be condemned.

This is the way the media plays with people's beliefs, by playing to their *emotions*. It's really simple and it is a formula that works.

Another way the media helps you decide what you will believe is through *disinformation*. This happens all the time in the daily press, and it was clearly on display during the event in which Jared

Loughner opened fire on a number of people including Congresswoman Giffords in Arizona a while back, as well as on a near-daily basis with respect to Mr. Obama.

The press is Obama's *willing* spokesperson and cheerleader. Instead of presenting the news in an unbiased manner, they cater to him. They do their best to present Obama as a seasoned individual capable of dealing with any matter of policy, foreign or domestic.

When they are unable to silence the critics, they simply resort to calling them names, a decidedly juvenile yet effective way of dispatching with those who disagree. This has been the norm for the talk show heads and pundits on the liberal side of the aisle who do not like Sarah Palin, or prefer to attack FOX News as being liars.

No news bureau is perfect of course, but it is interesting to see how many times these same liberal media outlets either lie outright or leave out some of the truth in one article after another. These ploys tend to create a perception and unfortunately, most buy into that perception, regardless of its efficacy.

It is as if the liberal, progressive side of the news is fighting hard to gain as many adherents as possible, so by denigrating those who disagree, they believe that more and more will come over to their side because that appears to be where the majority is now. Who wants to be in the minority? The most easily manipulated group of people happens to be young adults. They will go with something simply because it appears to be *rebellious*. Have we heard that before? Have other groups or individuals given in to the invitation to rebel? Of course. It is what beings and people with free wills do.

If people are told that some news bureau lies enough times, people will tend to believe it. If talking heads can find a way to make Mr. Obama look good time after time, then people will simply accept that as fact. It is far easier than a person doing his or her own research.

Record companies have always been pushing the envelope too, and they are doing so in greater degrees these days as well. I've talked about this in previous writings, but it is clear that Satan has placed individuals at specific key places in society with the talents they possess to create a pushing off place from what has been the norm.

Think of some of the artists that are praised today as misunderstood geniuses, or geniuses ahead of their time. Kirk Cobain, lead singer of the Seattle-based grunge band *Nirvanna*, who killed himself with a shotgun, was very famous for the lyrics he helped put to music. As the front man for *Nirvanna*, like most front men, he was the most well known in the group and also the most looked up to. Yet he was miserable and terribly misguided, in spite of his talent. People literally worship Kirk as some type of anti-hero.

Jim Morrison of the Doors, Janis Joplin, Jimi Hendrix, Jon Bonham, and too many others to name all died unnecessary deaths because they were willingly *used* by Satan to accomplish his goals. When he was done with them, he created a situation where either suicide or drug overdoses caused their death. Satan also knew how much they would be missed and worshipped, even in their death.

The music of yesterday – much of it seemingly harmless and easy-going – was born with deep roots within the drug culture. As people began experimenting more and more with drugs, the *"peace, love, dope"* motto became the experience of the 60s and 70s, eventually giving way to a culture of overdoses, alcoholism, and lyrical music that pushed the edge to redefine itself as something hard, nasty, and even savage. All of this has shaped the culture that exists today. Unfortunately, there is absolutely no going back.

What we are seeing today is a society of people being herded toward the same end. As the herd grows larger, more people want to become part of it. The problem, of course, is the herd is being directed toward a goal that most are really unaware of, but it does not seem to bother them because "everyone's" doing it. Their inner feelings of subjectivity tell them that everything is fine, because how could so many people be wrong?

It is going to be even more difficult to remain separate from the mainstream because it will become more forceful than ever and have no qualms about ostracizing those who are not part of that majority. It will take a very strong individual to stay disconnected. It will take an *authentic* Christian.

12

The New Age Alien

No one can deny that the subject of aliens has always been a hot and sometimes intense topic, but it seems to have come of age within the past decade or two. Though the chronology of the alien sightings, communication, and even abductions began with a deep sense of dread, things have progressed over the decades so that experiences related today by practitioners of esoteric arts are often far more mild and even described by many as *pleasurable* beyond anything they have experienced previously in this physical world. Moreover, there seems to be much more evidence that points to the fact that the entire acceptance of aliens has grown and has even taken on the form of a *science*.

A plethora of books, articles, and movies have been produced with a completely new emphasis. This new emphasis maintains that, unlike what people believed and indicated they experienced in the *past* through alleged contacts with aliens, the aliens of today seem more intent on helping humanity create a society that *advances* well beyond its current perceived limits.

Looking again through my library of books on the subject of aliens, I am reminded of the individuals who firmly believe that what they claim to routinely *experience* has been accomplished with the help of kind and benevolent beings who are not of this world. Depending upon which aspect of the New Age movement a person identifies with, these beings, as pointed out in earlier chapters, might be called *ascended masters*, *spirit guides*, *archangels*, or *aliens*.

Normally people involved in the esoteric arts adopt a form of New Ageism that *suits* them; one of the "benefits" of the New Age as I've mentioned before. There is something for everyone and everyone fits into some area. This is undoubtedly the mandate that Satan has given his minions; to create individual profiles within the New Age occult system that offers categories for each individual.

It is because of this mandate that the many highly developed and faceted avenues within the New Age exist. The detail-specific boundaries that separate each sub-category of New Ageism also serve to offer proof as to its other-worldly origins. In other words, it is that fully detailed web of deceit that makes up the New Age (which includes *all* esoteric groups and societies) which provides to the world a type of proof as to its efficacy and veracity. People have an easier time believing something that appears to them to be so multi-faceted that it could not have simply been made up. Compare that to Christianity and what do you have?

I'm sure for those who do not believe in an actual being named Satan who at one time was God's highest created being (according to Isaiah

14 and Ezekiel 27), the idea that there are those of us who believe he *does* exist is off-putting and naïve. That's life. Jesus understood Satan's reality, so I'm in very good company in also accepting the fact that Satan exists and his job is to torment and deceive. Ultimately, he has busied himself to keep people from receiving salvation and hopes to overthrow God one day. He will have some success on the former and fail miserably in the latter.

In my research for this book, I have obviously been studying God's Word as well as researching what other authors are saying. One thing I have found is that there is much agreement about what Satan does and why he does it, at least among many conservative scholars of the Bible.

The world is on a completely different track, however. To them, not only is Satan *not* real, but the idea of a being or entity like him who really has it in for humanity is laughable. The irony is that these same people who laugh themselves silly over the idea of an actual being named Satan find no difficulty whatsoever in believing in aliens that are here to help humanity.

Truth be told, I believe that beings masquerading as aliens actually *do* exist. I simply believe those beings to be *demonic* in origin. I have written other books that detail their origin as I believe is related in the Bible. I know, I know. Some of you may be laughing right now, but the reality is that twenty to thirty years ago, if you mentioned aliens in a serious conversation you would either have been stared at as if you were one yourself, or someone had their hand on the phone ready to dial the boys over at the rubber jacket factory. The only saving grace was to pass it off as a joke. No need to do so anymore.

Nevertheless, there is something interesting that all these alleged aliens are relating to humanity that bears a very close resemblance to *religion*; not good news for atheists and agnostics. The one good point for these folks is that to hear aliens tell it, God is not a Being, but a *mindset* or *office*. In fact, this office is something that can be obtained not by one specific individual, but by *many*.

Satan's plan has always been to get people to take the shortcut. Adam and Eve were doing fine until he showed up and pushed them over the edge with desire (cf. Genesis 2). It was a desire that said, *"No, we don't need to do it God's way! We can do it OUR way and still get there!"* They were wrong. We all would have done the same thing though, so we can't look down our noses at Adam and Eve as if we would have not followed the same path. Segue to 2011 and Satan is still trying to get the world to do it their own way – by taking his shortcuts.

I believe that in the garden, it is very likely that both Adam and Eve lived *fourth* dimensionally, and we touched on this in a previous chapter. They enjoyed the benefits of living that was not confined to our current three dimensions. Can I prove that? No, I can't, but please note that the only thing Satan could tempt them with was *godhood,* and he had an extremely narrow channel to work with in order to gain their trust. Today, that channel of influence is exponentially greater because of just how detailed and deceptive all avenues of the New Age have become.

Adam and Eve had everything they could have wanted, except the fruit of the tree of knowledge of good and evil. They walked with God in the cool of the Garden. They fellowshipped with Him on a daily basis, face to face. Nothing was hidden. They ruled over Creation, even the animals, including the birds of the air and fish of the sea. It seems to me that some way to communicate with those animals must have existed. Either all creatures understood whatever language Adam and Eve originally spoke, or they were able to get their desires across to the creatures in another way. How else would they have been able to *rule* Creation unless animals listened and obeyed?

When Adam and Eve *chose* to agree with Satan that his way was better than God's, they sinned and everything they had enjoyed *vanished*; some of it immediately, and some of it over time. Their health, their wellbeing, the way they gathered or cultivated food, and everything else associated with their lives in a perfect environment began to go away.

This in and of itself is proof enough that the current push toward global peace is simply a pipedream. It is not achievable by fallen human beings. Even if it was possible, it would not last, simply because people are *fallen*.

Sin is sin and that sin has affected every aspect of Creation. People exist today who are greedy beyond measure. All they think about is how to gain their next million.

The Sultan of Brunei has somewhere in the neighborhood of 7,000 cars and his estimated net worth is $20 billion dollars. The Sultan's main palace costs $350 million (in U.S.) dollars to build and boasts of 1788 rooms, 257 bathrooms and the total floor area is 2,152,782 sq. feet. He is only one of many who have wealth beyond measure, but do they have *salvation*?

When a person has that much wealth and uses it to satisfy his or her own pleasures, it is clear that what is important to them is taking care of *self*. While they may help the poor and/or homeless, they are giving out of their wealth and excess and as such, what they give away does not even cause the slightest ripple throughout their fortune.

In just one other example, Qaboos Bin Said, the Sultan of Oman, has royal properties worth $1.1 billion. The 67-year-old Sultan gained the throne after overthrowing his father. What a nice guy! Don't want to be second banana to anyone, especially your own father, anymore? No problem, just overthrow him! Get rid of him and take his wealth and whatever belongs to him. Make it your own.

Greed born of jealousy is the one thing that gives rise to many other problems. It was greed that caused Adam and Eve to succumb to the Tempter's suggestions. They wanted what they could not have, so by listening to the Temper, they were able to acquire it, but it cost them and the rest of humanity dearly.

Think of it. Satan snared our first parents because he highlighted what they did not *have*. He made it sound plausible to have the fruit of the tree of knowledge of good and evil.

Had Adam and Eve *not* succumbed to the Tempter, their lives would have remained as they were with the added benefit of never again being tempted to do evil. They would have passed the test and God would have granted them eternal life.

It is the same with us today, except of course we have no *experiential* knowledge of what it is like to *not* sin. We were born in sin and we continue to live in sin now. Even as Christians, our sin nature remains firmly attached and will need to be surgically removed upon our death. Sin is never that far away from us.

So when Satan went to our first parents, he helped them believe that they did not have to do things the way God had instructed in order to become *gods* themselves. This was defined by Satan as knowing the difference between *good and evil*. Again, they may have already been living fourth dimensionally (I'm making an educated guess here because of their ability to rule over all Creation - animals, plants, everything), which meant that there were things they did that we cannot do now and they were *unable* to continue doing *after* they fell.

People do not now live fourth dimensionally. We live in three dimensions and we are stuck with that until we die. Once death takes us, we will go through that door into eternity where the Lord will give us new glorified bodies, capable of handling dimensions beyond our current three. I believe that if our bodies were somehow able to experience anything beyond our current three dimensions, they would explode or be destroyed some other way. Our sinfully corrupt bodies simply are not currently able to handle moving beyond three dimensions. These sin-encased physical forms we live in are well below the original beauty of God's created order and design. We will need new bodies to endure and appreciate dimensions beyond our three.

So what is Satan's lie now? It's still "ye shall be gods," however for humanity now, the carrot hung over our heads is slightly different and attempts to help us believe that if we try hard enough now, if we meditate often enough now, if we perform enough goodwill (good works) toward humanity now, then we have an excellent chance of being able to live in the fourth dimension. Once we are able to live in the fourth dimension, we live...ready? ... as gods!

The fourth dimension is the dimension that we – as human beings who live in three dimensions with sin-marred physical bodies – *cannot* access. In general, the fourth dimension (as well as anything else beyond our three dimensions that is built into the universe with which we exist) is off-limits to us until *after* we die.

Once our first parents fell, it was as if God cordoned off anything beyond our three dimensions. He closed and sealed that door, forbidding us to go looking for it. This is one of the reasons why we are forbidden to seek the advice of mediums and spirit guides. First, it is spiritual adultery, and second, God has fenced us in making those areas now off-limits completely. He knows that going beyond our three dimensions would destroy us because our fallen bodies are not able to exist outside our three dimensions. Spiritual adultery is seeking after something that is not allowed. It is disobedience, also known as rebellion, also known as sin.

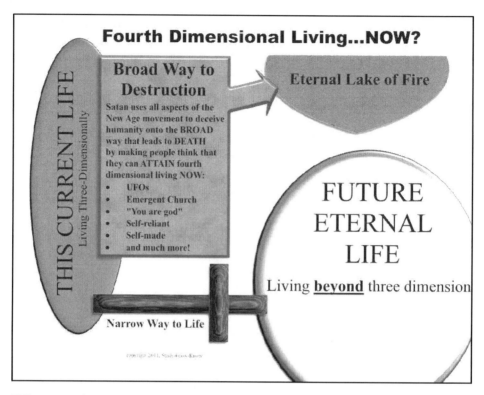

When we die, our soul leaves our earthly bodies, and we are given new, glorified bodies that are perfectly capable of living beyond our three dimensions. As stated, I believe the fourth dimension (and others) was available to both Adam and Eve *prior* to their fall. I also believe that is where all of humanity was intended to live by God, from the moment of Creation onward throughout all eternity. The fall interrupted that by cutting us off from all but the three dimensions we now live in (for our own safety), which is all our fallen physical bodies can handle. Going beyond these dimensions is something Satan wants us to believe we *can* do and he is more than willing to help us believe that fourth dimensional living is attainable *now*, in our present state.

But God has literally boxed us in for our own protection. He has created a fenced-in area that keeps us where we are supposed to be in order to remain *alive*. It is possible that when God spoke of cordoning off the tree of life in the Garden of Eden, the tree itself was actually in another dimension, one that eventually closed itself off from entrance by Adam and Eve and any other human beings.

I believe it's also possible that the reason Nimrod wanted people to build a tower to the heavens is because there was something in his fallen DNA (as possibly one of the Nephilim) that remembered a location to another dimension that would have expanded ancient humanity's world beyond the three dimensions to which God had sequestered humanity.

For the longest time, humanity has wanted to fly like the bird. We have created all sorts of air and spacecraft that gets us off this planet. Is there something deep within us that remembers the time we were actually able to flit and float from one dimension to another with ease? We really do not know a great deal about what Adam and Eve experienced before they fell, do we? Reading through the *Book of Enoch* gives us a glimpse into what may have been the natural and normal existence of Adam and Eve prior to their fall.

The Bible tells us that Enoch walked with God (Genesis 5). He was considered righteous. The Bible also tells us that *"And Enoch walked with God after he begat Methuselah three hundred years, and begat sons and daughters: And all the days of Enoch were three hundred sixty and five years: And Enoch walked with God: and he was not; for God took him"* (Genesis 5:22-24). I find it fascinating that though the rest of the people were living to ages of 700 to over 900 years, Enoch, who was considered righteous by God (and he walked with Him), only lived to be three hundred sixty-five years of age. The text tells us that God took Enoch. Apparently, Enoch did not die, but was simply translated directly to heaven.

From Genesis 5, we do not really know what it means when we are told that Enoch walked with God. Obviously, there was some sort of spiritual connection and it was clearly Enoch's desire (surely placed there by God Himself) to seek God. Reading the *Book of Enoch* fills in some of the details, if it is authentic. There is no real indication that the *Book of Enoch* was inspired by the Holy Spirit as were the other books that make up the Bible. However, this also does not mean that simply because it may not have been inspired, it is therefore not true. To arrive at that conclusion is absurd. That is like saying a commentary that a person spent half their life writing on the Bible or parts of the Bible is of no value, simply because it was not inspired as the Bible is inspired.

There was something extraordinary about Enoch's life and the glimpse that we see in Scripture tells me that Enoch's walk with God may have been similar to Moses' walk with God, though not as great. Moses of course was used by God to lead the captive Israelites out of Egypt in order to form the nation of Israel.

Like Enoch, Adam and Eve undoubtedly existed in a realm that is long gone. I recall talking with one couple about the Garden of Eden and the wife asked me point blank, "*Do you think it's still there?*" I was a bit dumbfounded because the obvious and immediate answer is "*No, it's not there due to the Flood.*" It amazes me how people get caught up on one idea at times, chasing logic out the window.

If Adam and Eve experienced life in more dimensions than we currently do, but our DNA might "remember" it though we ourselves cannot experience it now, then it makes sense to me that Satan would create a plan so multi-faceted and so detailed, based on aliens from other worlds or dimensions, in order to pique our interest. Remember, he is trying to tap into what may be deeply resident within us and he knows exactly what Adam and Eve experienced prior to the fall because he was there and saw it.

If he knows what Adam and Eve actually experienced before they sinned and fell, why would he not try to make us believe that we can even now regain what was lost? Is it impossible to believe that Satan would work hard to replicate for us what Adam and Eve experienced, only doing so in our minds? Of course, the experience in our minds would have to be so realistic that it would be easily thought to be *reality*. Is Satan powerful enough to do this? It seems clear from Scripture that this is the case.

For instance, the idea that people can use astral project to send their souls into space and other realms is not a new concept. It has been around for some time. However, it is only within the past twenty years or so that the idea has found its way seriously into the mainstream of society. People routinely write books on their alleged capability of flying through the multitude of layers within our universe. Are those experiences true? Did they actually occur? I cannot imagine that they did because those dimensions are completely off limits to humanity. Our bodies could not handle it because of what the fall has done to our physical bodies and even our minds. Moreover, our souls cannot leave our bodies unless and until we die. We cannot actually send our souls flying free from our earthly tents to sojourn through time and/or space. Yet, could Satan and his cronies create such a realistic "inner" episode that rivals anything real in our physical world? I believe that he is perfectly capable of doing so, with God's permission.

If these other dimensions beyond our three are off limits to humanity, then what is happening? What is actually taking place when people say that aliens have taken them somewhere? What has occurred when people say that God sent them to hell or heaven or both for 90 minutes? What is going on? If these dimensions are off limits to us, then why are more and more people making bold claims to the contrary?

Obviously, I'm going to say that what is happening is the result of a huge, fully dynamic counterfeit to the reality that does exist beyond our dimensions. Satan lives there. He saw what humanity experienced in the Garden of Eden. He knows full well that deep within our souls, we long to regain what once was ours. He also knows that this particular reality cannot occur until *after* death, but he is not going to tell us that. He will lie while creating things our minds dream of experiencing. It is as simple as that.

Even Paul, when he experienced the vision of the third heaven (cf. 1 Corinthians), did not know if it was an out of body experience or a vision. It was so real to him that it was difficult to distinguish the experiential facts surrounding the event.

In the book of Revelation, either the apostle John saw what appeared to be complete visions of the future in his mind, or God literally took him to heaven to see it firsthand. If the former, then it is clear that the vision itself was extremely realistic. If the latter, then God protected his body from corruption and destruction when taken out of these three dimensions while he saw what God was going to do in the future. There are many times when John states he was "*taken in spirit*" out of the body or to the throne of God, etc., in the book of Revelation.

We know from Satan's track record in Scripture that he wants more than anything for as many people as possible to attempt to circumvent God's prescribed will for their life. He does not want people to become authentically saved. That's the last thing he wants and to that end, he has created a lie that is so vast and so multi-layered that the lie itself appears to be absolutely real. Because of that, distinction for most cannot be made between the falsehood he has created and reality that exists.

Satan knows all too well that people cannot leave our three dimensions for any others. We are at present not built that way. However, that does not stop him from his attempts to replicate those dimensions with as much reality as possible *in a person's mind*. While I am aware that some people have had items implanted in their bodies, those things are easily done by Satan as well.

Think of how easily Satan created a tornado that took the lives of Job's children (cf. Job 1). Consider how Satan was able to gather troops to rise against Job's servants and to take what belonged to Job. Here is a being that has retained much of his original power with only his loyalty simply change sides from God to himself. We have no true understanding of what Satan is capable of doing, but it would appear from the glimpses we are given in Scripture that he has *tremendous* power and ability.

Could he use this power to create a reality for people that, while that reality may actually exist in one form or another, does not involve taking people *into* that reality? Could he not simply recreate that reality, or even create a powerful *lie* that appears to be real, in someone's brain? I believe he can easily do so and the more people who seek after this type of experience, the better he is able to create it because he now has their *cooperation*, whether they recognize that or not.

In Job 7, Job briefly describes the hallucinations he experienced at the hand of Satan. As he cried out to God, he said, *"Then thou scarest me with dreams, and terrifiest me through visions: So that my soul chooseth strangling, and death rather than my life"* (Job 7:14-15). If Job became so afraid that he wanted death rather than life, the dreams and visions that terrified him must have been traumatic to say the least! What he saw we do not know, but it was realistic.

I firmly believe that many of the horror movies that have been produced have originated not in people's brains, but with Satan's ideas; ideas he then *planted* in the brains of people who could make them happen. Think of some of the movies that have been produced within the past few years. Many of these movies blur the line completely between good and evil and often promote evil as good. Beyond this, the amount of gore and fright has exponentially increased over time, leaving little to nothing to the imagination. With the rise of digital special effects, nearly anything that can be imagined can be created for the screen.

Years ago, a "jump" scene was when someone or something jumped out from nowhere, scaring the audience with a jump. That's passe now and nothing short of gore-filled scenes will satisfy anymore.

More movies being made today deal with the supernatural, zombies, the devil himself, fallen angels, good angels, demons, and the like. People are getting so used to seeing these images on the screen that it would probably surprise very few if they ran into the actual beings on the street some day.

Where exactly do these filmmakers obtain their images for the beings and entities they bring to life on the screen? Where else could they possibly come from except from the beings themselves who exist in other dimensions? Whether they look like that or not is really not the point. The point is that these beings know how to scare human beings.

A number of years ago, a movie called *The Devil's Advocate* was produced, starring Al Pacino. The film portrayed Pacino as Satan, who turns out to be the father of Keanu Reeve's character, Kevin Lomax. I watched it because I wanted to see exactly how the supernatural would be portrayed. I knew people in the special effects industry in Hollywood and was also able to learn how some of those effects were done.

There were a few scenes that stuck out in my mind from the movie. One of them was when one of the women in the movie was trying on dresses with a friend. The first woman was either possessed or demonized. While she was talking to the friend, invisible hands started moving all over her body and the indentations those hands made on her skin became obvious.

In one other scene, a man in the law firm (the entire movie revolved around a particular law firm) had outlived his usefulness and while jogging through Central Park one afternoon, he was attacked by two indigent men. During the attack, their faces changed from human-looking to absolutely demonic. The effect was seamless, and I learned later it was done largely with remote-control masks the actors wore during the scene. From watching the movie, no one would have guessed that this is how it was accomplished. It simply appeared that the true identity of beings that motivated the homeless men snuck through into our reality or dimension for just a moment.

Science tells us that we only use roughly ten percent of our brain at most. If this is true, then what about the other ninety percent that is *not* being used? Does Satan have access to it directly or indirectly? Can he send images into parts of our brain that will appear to be extremely real, that people react to as if they *are* real?

I recently marveled at the quality of animation with the movie *Tangled*. When I was a kid animation was good because there were enough still image frames per second to create what appeared to be smooth action on the screen. As time progressed, cartoons and animation in general became much more jerky in movement in style. This was done to save money (using fewer frames) and for no other reason.

Enter the age of digital filmmaking. Movies like *Star Wars* and others broke ground with startling special effects. This made it possible to do things inside a computer that cost far less than to have a master modelmaker build a miniature set. While miniatures still needed to be built and used for filming, digital effects made it possible to achieve quality film sequences without spending a ton of money and also made it far safer for actors and stunt people.

However, even those early effects compared to what is now able to be produced pale in comparison. Early on, it was difficult at best to create realistic-looking water or fire sequences, for instance. That is now a thing of the past, as can be clearly seen in any number of recent animated movies. The quality and realism is nothing less than breathtaking.

Even facial expressions and nuances in animated movies have improved to such a degree that it will not be long before Hollywood will be able to make a movie with actors that have long died, simply voiced by an impersonator. I recently watched one segment of a new DC video game my son had purchased online. The quality was remarkable and it would not have been difficult at all to watch an entire hour and a half movie done in that mode due to the realism. The characters' mouths did not simply move up and down, or open and close, but taking the time to watch the lips move, it is easy to see that the producers and animators actually have the mouths move to *form* the words that the characters are saying as they are voiced by actors.

Animation is becoming the new reality in many circles. Movies are routinely produced in 3-D today, which is nothing like the 3-D of my day growing up. Not long ago, I went to a store and saw a clip of a Sci-Fi space series being broadcast in 3-D. The glasses are far different from my childhood and the result is that the 3-D literally comes off the screen. There are *layers* to what is seen too, which is much different than the 3-D of yesteryear.

Holograms are also becoming much more detailed and lifelike. There seems to be no end to where technology is taking this planet and all of it, though neutral or innocuous in and of itself, is being used and will continue to be used by the enemy of our souls to bring about realistic-looking miracles that will be seen around the globe by everyone as they occur.

Certainly, it is safe to say that our brains are being unlocked like never before. Mankind is achieving what only a few decades ago seemed impossible. It is difficult for my son to understand that personal computers have only been around since the mid-to-late 80s to any great degree.

I recall working at a computer store long ago when games were text-based. They also plugged into the computer via a cord connected to a cassette tape recorder. Computers were DOS-based (disc operation system) then as well. When Windows got into the game, things changed in a big way, with the introduction of the mouse and "point and click" technology.

That first version of Windows 3.1 was amazing, yet today is considered a dinosaur. Things have changed so quickly that it is impossible to keep up.

Not long ago, I needed to purchase a new desktop computer. At the checkout they asked if I wanted to purchase the three-year maintenance plan. My answer was a simple "no," because in eight months or less, the computer I was purchasing for over $600 would be outmoded compared to what was then going to be available.

Everything that we have today due to technology stems from the fact that humankind is creating like never before. Technology is leading the way to a better world in many ways, yet will ultimately never be able to solve mankind's problems. These are only solved by God. However, Satan wants us to believe that the better the technology, the quicker problems will be solved. In fact, I believe this push to greater technological advances simply plays into the enemy's hands. He will at the end of the day use it for his gains and advantages. I firmly believe that he is busy using technolgy now to achieve his end of creating realities for people that they believe will give them even greater measures of success later on. This is all a *misdirect* on Satan's part, though. While there is nothing wrong with technology, it can and certainly is being used to compromise a general belief in God and to place mankind on the pedestal of greatness.

There are many examples of aliens discussing aspects of technology with people. It is fascinating to see just how deep Satan and his followers will go in fabricating and spreading the lies that people routinely accept as truth in this day and age. This includes causing people to believe that fourth dimension living is available now. Advances in technolgy bring people to the realization that fourth dimension living is within our reach. Centuries ago (and even decades ago), this would not have been considered or believed that strongly. Not so today.

Fourth dimension living *will* occur for authentic Christians, but it will not occur in this life. It will only happen after this life is over and after we have traded in our fallen, corrupt body for a new, unadulterated body that God will give us in the afterlife.

God's plan for getting us back to living *beyond* our three dimensions is called the plan of salvation. It is through Jesus that we become born again, or born from above (cf. John 3). Being born again gives us a new nature in this life and a new body to match (minus the sin nature) in the next.

There is absolutely no way to get to that point – living beyond our current three dimensions – as long as we are *alive* in this dimension. Living fourth dimensionally (and beyond) is only for the next life, since this current state of existence is severely marred and handicapped by sin and the resident sin nature with each and every person. Salvation is the only true path to that life and the door that leads us to it is the door of death. When we die, we pass to the next life. It is there we live the fulfillment of eternal life that we received here. This is not to say that salvation does not benefit us in this life, because it does. It is to say that we do not enjoy all the benefits of salvation now. Much more is to come.

The same can be said of those who will spend eternity, by their choice, *apart* from God. As they live in this life, they remain fallen, fully marred by sin, with nothing within them that begins the redemptive process. These people do not have the Holy Spirit living within them, indwelling them, recreating Christ's character, or letting them enjoy any of the benefits of salvation *now*. They are dead, *spiritually*. When they physically die, their *eternal* death will officially begin as they are cast from God's presence forever and ever. So in the same sense, people who are dead spiritually *here* will realize the full import of their decision against receiving salvation. Once they pass from this life to the next, the clear understanding of their rejection of Jesus will become absolutely and unequivocally clear. They may have what they consider to be a decent life here. They may be relatively happy and content (by the world's standards). They may be hard-working individuals who have gained much in this life. But without God, they have absolutely nothing. Whatever they think they had in this life will be gone forever.

Paul tells us in Romans that the entire Creation groans under the heavy load of sin (cf. Romans 1 and following). This situation will not fully be rectified until after Jesus reigns for 1,000 years on this planet and then destroys this heaven and earth, creating new ones to take their place. That is God's plan and it will be carried out.

Living in the fourth dimension and beyond is living that is only gifted to those who trust in the Name of Jesus Christ as Savior and Lord. Those who believe that Jesus died for sinful humanity, opening a way back to God for those who seek Him, will be rewarded with eternal life. Eternal life is living with God, physically, beyond these current three dimensions. God is not bound or limited by our three dimensions. He is infinite. We are finite. We have been segregated to three dimensions due to our rebellion and sin. Satan is doing his best to make us believe that we can gain access to other dimensions beyond our three by meditating, performing good works toward all humanity, and believing that we are gods. Too many people fall for that and die into eternity already spiritually dead. They will awaken to a horror they can hardly imagine.

There is no shortcut to salvation. Faith is required and faith is exercised when people humble themselves in realizing that Christ died for the ungodly. They begin to understand that salvation is a free gift, and it is given to those who ask for it in humility. A person who asks God for salvation does so because he/she realizes his/her need for God. They realize they cannot do it themselves, and in fact are quite incapable of doing it at all.

The end result of the salvation leading to eternal life is living in glory with the Lord, forever, beyond these measly three dimensions. That type of living THEN will not be limited by the three dimensions we live in NOW.

Here's the rub though. Even though it is impossible because God has walled off dimensions beyond our three, Satan has worked very hard to spell out a way for people to obtain fourth dimensional living now. We do not have to wait until we die, he says through any number of teachings and tenets. We can begin to work toward it now, as we live. His lies teach that once we have worked hard enough, we gain access to that fourth dimension, which frees us from the confines of our current three dimensions. In doing so, we take on the attributes of a god, able to have mastery over the dimensions, no longer confined by them.

This is of course a complete fabrication, at least according to the Bible (and if I could, I would buy stock in the Bible due to its veracity and truthfulness!). God says there is only one way back to Him and that is through Jesus. Satan says there are many paths and none of them go through Jesus at all (though he pretends that Jesus is part of it).

It seems all too clear to me. Satan wants human beings to believe that fourth dimensional living is real for people now. Once this is attained, it is the same as living divinely. God says that we cannot access those other dimensions now and we should not try. Doing so is spiritual adultery, idolatry, and just plain sin due to disobedience to God's stated commands. We need to go through Him, receive the salvation He provided through Jesus, God the Son, and in the *next* life, other dimensions that God has kept from us now for our own good will be opened up to us.

People unknowingly buy into Satan's schemes because they *sound* good, it puts them in the driver's seat, and because they do not have to deal with the problem of *sin*. It's a shortcut that ends in death, not life. I hope you have made a decision to receive the only salvation that is available for you. There is no shortcut to eternal life. It goes through Jesus and Him alone!

13

Why the Message is Inviting

It is difficult to walk through this life seeing multitudes of people reject the only path that leads to life. On one hand, as authentic Christians, our hearts go out to these people. We know that if God had not opened *our* eyes to His truth, we would be as blind as they remain. At the same time, we also know that people are blind because they *wish* to be so. Paul makes this unequivocally clear in Romans chapter one.

There is a dual problem that *seems* unfair yet is completely fair if God is God, and He certainly is that. The problem has to do with the fact of the fall as well as the results of it.

We can argue back and forth about whether or not God truly loves people by allowing these same people to choose a path that guides them directly to hell. However, our debating about it would have absolutely no impact on the truth of the situation at all.

What's done is done and the reason humanity fell has solely to do with the fact that God created people with a *free will*. Does this mean God was wrong? As Paul would say, *heaven forbid!* There is absolutely no way that God can ever be said to be wrong about anything He does. It makes not one bit of difference whether puny humanity has the capacity to understand it or not. The only thing that matters is truth and that truth is only found in God.

Free will gave humanity the ability to choose. Included with that comes the potential to choose *the wrong path*. This is the way God designed it. When He created Adam and then Eve, He did so with the intent that they should have the opportunity to decide for themselves whether they would deliberately and faithfully follow His commands, or choose their own path.

What our first parents failed to realize, of course, is that free will never places a person in the position of being able to choose to follow *no one*. Free will allows a person to choose one thing or the other; God or Satan.

God made humanity, placed them in the Garden of Eden and gave them one simple rule. It wasn't complicated. It was very clear, in spite of the fact that Eve *added* to God's rule. She told the serpent that neither she nor her husband were to *touch* the forbidden fruit, something God had never said. He said they should not *eat* it.

The free will that brought about the desire to move *away* from God through *disobedience* is the same free will that would have allowed Adam and Eve to *remain* in the Garden through *obedience*. It seems then that there is a problem with free will, *not* with God.

It is funny if not ironic when people blame God for the existence of hell. The question constantly asked is: how could a loving God send people to hell? How could a loving God allow sin, death, pain, suffering, or any other negative into the world? He allowed it by virtue of the fact that He created human beings with the capacity to *choose*. He did not create automatons. He created living, breathing, thinking human beings who were given the ability to decide for themselves whom they would follow; God or Satan.

So when both Adam and Eve fell, they literally invited sin into the world. Everything changed. From that point onward, sin, sickness, death, greed, jealousy, murder, hatred, lying, stealing, raping, and everything else that is opposed to God came into being. Since mankind made a legally binding decision to do what they wanted to do and disobeyed God, how can God be assessed blame for anything that happened *after* that fact?

These people are saying that God should have stepped in and stopped Adam and Eve from making the terrible decision they made, yet these same individuals would say that free will should be allowed – but only for the good things apparently. They ask why there is so much evil in the world. How could God allow it? He allows it because humanity invited it by believing Satan's lie.

It *will* come to the end though. All of it will come to its final conclusion and through it all God will be seen as holy, sinless, perfect, loving, glorified, and much more. Nothing will remain that does not glorify God. Everything will give glory to Him, the Creator of all things. Every knee will bow.

Any creature that has the ability to choose seems to want to choose the path that goes *away from* and *against* God. Paul seems to hint at this when he refers to the *elect angels of God* in one of his letters to Timothy (cf. 1 Timothy 5:21). It would appear then that there are some angels who were specifically made by God to *remain* for all time and eternity as completely righteous, able only to do God's perfect will, 100% of the time. Other angels were created and given the ability to rebel against God, and this they did. These of course became the fallen angels of the Bible.

It is certainly interesting to consider the fact that angels who existed *without* sin in God's holy presence would one day opt to break away from Him *through* sin. In fact, it seems almost inconceivable. How could that happen, we wonder? How is that remotely possible? Yet it will happen again with multitudes of people at the end of the one thousand year reign of Jesus on this earth, according the closing chapters of the book of Revelation. Satan, who will have spent those same one thousand years locked away in the pit, will upon his release manage to persuade multitudes of people to turn away from Jesus and follow Satan. We learn this in Revelation 20:7-8, which tells us, *"And when the thousand years are expired, Satan shall be loosed out of his prison, And shall go out to deceive the nations which are in the four quarters of the earth, Gog, and Magog, to gather them together to battle: the number of whom is as the sand of the sea."*

In spite of the fact that these people lived under the fully righteous rule of Jesus for up to ten centuries, in the end a multitude of people so large that the number was like the sand of the sea will gather *with* Satan in one last coup attempt! How can that be? That can't be right, can it? Yet there it is in Scripture, written ahead of time so that when it happens it will simply be one more proof that the Bible is true and God is holy, righteous, and just.

Is it that much different from the situation surrounding Adam and Eve, who lived in *perfection* and also *without* sin, yet one day opted to follow their own desires, rejecting God? The pattern seems to be that those creatures given the ability to choose unilaterally use it at some point to snub God and, in rebellion to Him, simply walk away.

What could Satan have possibly said to the angels that would have caused them to think that following *him* was better than remaining with God? How could Adam and Eve have possibly been motivated to walk away from God, given the circumstances in which they lived prior to the fall?

Is free will so strong that it will bring down even the strongest individual? It would seem so, wouldn't it? Free will – such as it is – seems to want to always and only profit *self*. The only individual who has ever managed to remain free of the downward pull of free will is Jesus Himself. Thank God for that, because without His perseverance in remaining true to God the Father, we would not have ever had the way back to God opened to us again through the only salvation that is available to humanity.

The desire to be something we are not seems to be part of the package that we call free will. Satan had everything he could have ever hoped to have. The highest created being, who likely led the heavenly choir, was robed in majesty and had responsibility and authority above all others except God Himself. Yet this individual eventually chafed at being simply *created* and having to do the dictates of Another. He somehow convinced one-third of the angelic host to follow him in rebellion. They too, it seems, recoiled at the idea that they were created, and as such, were beholden to a Being who far exceeded their abilities. They apparently believed that by following Satan, they would be able to come out from under God's rule.

Both Adam and Eve, although living peaceful lives, with nothing to fear from God's Creation, soon succumbed to the belief that in spite of the fact that they were also created beings, they too could distance themselves from their Creator and see and call themselves *gods*.

If individuals who were without sin could give into the temptation to see themselves as more than they were, how much more difficult is it for us – born into this world as *fallen* people with activated sinful natures – to remain free from the dictates that our free will creates? There seems little chance of avoiding the selfish demands of our free will. In the end, it does not seem that we are actually *free*, does it?

Satan experienced free will. He fell. Some of the angels enjoyed it. They fell. Adam and Eve lived by it. They fell. We are born with it, *already* fallen. Free will does not appear to be a good thing for created beings. Is that one of the things that God is showing the universe?

Certainly those who arrive in heaven after death will have the sin nature removed and with it, the free will. At that point, the only desires left will be to glorify God in every possible way for all of eternity. Never again will people have the thought or desire to do something that is *against* God. Never will anyone seek his or her own welfare, but will instead consider only what is best for God and others. It is something that is nearly impossible to envision now.

Think of the millions and millions of people in this world who live *now*. Then think of the trillions and trillions of people who have lived since Adam and Eve. All of these people were born with an activated sin nature that constantly urges our free will (corrupt as it is) to act *against* God and *for* ourselves.

All of us have chafed under the burden of that activated sin nature and free will that leans toward self and away from God. Even if our free will was as *pure* as Adam's and Eve's, it seems clear enough that we also would fall. Paul says as much in Romans (cf. 3:23; 5:12). In Adam's place, we would have done the exact same thing that he did.

Is the desire to be *god* so strong that we are not willing to share that deity with anyone else, much less the One who created us in the first place? Is it that, or is it the fact that our free will is such that it will ultimately not allow us to remain "shackled" to anyone for any length of time?

Of course the problem with free will and our sin nature is that we become completely blind to what is true and right. We are still accountable even though blind. Paul also speaks of this in Romans (cf. Romans 5).

Is the message of the New Age, along with aliens, ascended masters, spirit guides or whatever else they may be called, so inviting because by heeding it we erroneously believe that becoming "god" absolves us of all *guilt*? It is certainly a far more inviting way to enter into a perfected state of living, isn't it? Who wants to have to deal with the *facts* of the matter: that humanity fell in Adam and because of that, death is the result?

Adam and Eve gave into Satan for their own reason and they did so in spite of the fact that they had not *yet* sinned. Desiring to be gods was not necessarily sought after to *cover* or *expunge* their guilt since they had not yet done anything wrong. This is not the case with people today who chase after the fabrications of the New Age.

The desire of the average person today to be a god is for another reason entirely. I believe it is sought after in order to *assuage the guilt* that resides deeply within each individual. Unfortunately, this guilt continues to exist until such a time as God knows that the person is beyond their ability to respond to His calling.

There is a time when God gives people over to their deepest desires. He calls them. He woos them. He patiently and temporarily looks past their wrongdoings in order to give them opportunity to come to Him, and in so doing, He knows of course that by faith in Him, their sin will be canceled (cf. Romans 1).

He will do this as long as is necessary until it is clear that the person truly wants no part of Him. Sadly, sorrowfully, He will let them go their way, knowing full well that the way they have chosen does not lead away from Him necessarily. They will one day face Him in abject horror and terror from the hell that they find themselves in. They will do that with the additional horror of knowing that the same God who spent their life lovingly calling them to Him is now a God of wrath, pouring out His anger on them because of their sin for all *eternity*.

Satan would like us to believe that if we only embrace some inner deity, then we will move away from the guilt that is left over from the ancient past and has no place in the present. Embracing our inner divinity allows us to move closer to God, so we are led to believe.

The truth, of course, is far different. Not only do we end up embracing a complete lie, but we move further and further away from God, who is love, to find ourselves united with God who hates sin; something that unsaved people will fully become in eternity.

What people need to see is that all this talk of *aliens, reptilian shape shifters, Pleadians, Grays*, and other entities is all a *game*. It does not exist. It is a multi-leveled paradox perpetrated on unsuspecting humanity in order to keep us from receiving God's love, through which comes the only true salvation.

People are not guiltless. We cannot say with any truth that God is unfair. We get what we deserve. Though God loves His Creation, He has shown that He is willing to destroy parts of it that bring Him no glory. That is the root of the problem. In this world, all people are given the opportunity to glorify God or themselves. Those who for one reason or another choose self will be destroyed. Those who respond to God's call, opting to follow Him wherever He leads, will gain life. It is as simple as that, yet Satan has introduced a house of mirrors into the equation so that it *appears* to be far more complex.

14

Upcoming Scenarios

I am always fascinated with what people are willing to believe. Many will believe just about anything if it comes to them with some sort of authority. These individuals view that authority as proof enough and believe they need nothing further, in spite of the fact that deep within them, something may be telling them to avoid and ignore what they are being tempted to believe.

This is just the case within the New Age and especially in the area of *aliens*. The world seems to be so open to the idea that aliens may well exist that they are willing to throw caution to the wind in their search for answers leading to some perceived truth. The problem of course is that the answers they find are rarely born of truth. While truth is mixed in with the answers they find, that truth is not complete because it lies alongside error. This doesn't bother people, though, because they have learned to go by *feelings* as opposed to *logic* or *intuition*; not that either of these is a perfect guard against falsehoods, but they often serve their purpose as the first line of defense.

I have spent many hours on the Internet viewing videos of people who claim to be mediums. These individuals routinely enter into trances (or appear to do so) and present the teachings of their familiar spirit (forbidden by Scripture; Leviticus 19:31; Deuteronomy 18:10-13; Acts 16:16-18) to viewers.

Much has been written about what these entities from beyond tell people, and it seems interesting to say that most do not make the connection between the message and the messenger. If people actually took the time to understand what was being foisted upon them, they might wonder why so many messages appear to be so similar and why almost all of them deal with aspects of a religious nature. Aside from authentic Christians and a few secular researchers, these questions are never asked by the average individual.

One of the most enlightening aspects of the message that is often transmitted from beyond our dimension has to do with what will occur in the future. For instance, the Bible speaks of a number of events that are yet future. These events have come under great attack by liberal biblical scholars. Whether it is the idea that Jesus will physically reign for one thousand years on the planet, with His headquarters in Jerusalem, or whether an event known as the Rapture will actually occur is being debated more than ever today.

Rarely does it seem that people step back to look at the big picture. Those within Christendom argue and debate the veracity of such events like the Rapture with much rancor and vitriol. This is tragic, but I believe it is one of the ways in which the enemy gains the upper hand in matters of theology and doctrine. If he can cause Christians (professing and authentic) to be at each other's throats over aspects of theology, then he has certainly won a small temporary battle.

Christians who spend their time arguing about the Rapture or Tribulation, for instance, are not likely involved in evangelizing the people of this world who do not yet have salvation. I have been there myself, wasting time debating aspects of Eschatology (study of the end times or last days), until the Lord helped me realize that it amounts to nothing since most people who enter any debate already have their minds made up about their position.

Satan knows this and excels at creating environments that pit Christian against Christian. Not too long ago, it became in vogue to refer to Christians like myself who believe in the PreTrib Rapture as heretical. This is apparently because (it is said) when the Rapture does not occur prior to the Tribulation, then my bubble will burst, creating such a trauma within me that I will be blind to the reality of the Antichrist and will take the mark of the beast, mistaking the Antichrist for Jesus Christ. The absurdity of such a view is clearly seen, yet it persists.

The reality is that if the Rapture does not occur prior to the Tribulation as I believe it will, then I will be clearly *wrong* in my belief. If I am alive at that time when the Tribulation begins, the idea that I will somehow become so stupefied with blindness that I will not understand the difference between Antichrist and Jesus is equally irrational.

Is God able to protect His own? Of course! However, some apparently believe that He is unable to do that and that I will be left to my own devices.

Yet, while this argument continues unabated within Christian circles, all one has to do is look beyond Christian circles to the New Age to learn what Satan is telling his followers in that realm. While he is busy pitting Christian against Christian within Christendom, he seems to be telling New Agers a completely different story. Let's take a moment or two to learn what is being taught within the New Age regarding the concept of the Rapture.

The world is moving onward, seemingly without a care in the world, with the exception of the economy and the continued peace talks in the Middle East. Most believe that these things will work themselves out in time, so they are not too terribly troubled by them. After all, economic cycles, weather patterns and the like come and go, they say. What is interesting though is what is going on in the world *below* the surface. I don't mean in the dirt. I mean *behind the scenes*.

Many Christians today look forward to an event known in the Bible as the Rapture. The Rapture, spoken about by Paul and implied through the teachings of Christ, is the event in which all who are part of the invisible Church – both living and deceased – are raised to meet Christ in the air (cf. I Thessalonians 4:13-18). Paul's closing words in this section indicate that this occurs in order to avoid the "wrath to come."

Of course, there are growing numbers of Christians who do not at all believe in the Rapture. They look at it as a contrivance by other Christians who are simply afraid to face trials and tribulations. The problem with this reasoning is that it does not take into account the trials and tribulations that occur *daily* in life. Many Christians throughout the world are undergoing severe trials and persecution. Many have lost their lives because of this. Others will likely follow down that path of martyrdom. The argument that the Rapture is simply an "escape clause" really has no merit. Certainly, the truth of a doctrine is not decided on whether or not it seems *plausible*. The truth of it is either confirmed or not in Scripture alone.

Many Christians have spent a good deal of time discussing and arguing over the possibility of the Rapture, leaning on this verse or that to prove or disprove it. At the end of such arguments, people are usually no closer to changing their viewpoints, because both parties firmly believe that they are correct in their belief.

The Bible is the best resource to look to when attempting to discern any doctrine espoused. The true test should always be what is found in God's Word. However, at the same time, with so many people seeing the same passages teaching two different things, it helps to go outside the Bible to see if any verification can be found for such a doctrine as the Rapture.

In a chapter of one of my previous works titled *The Anti-Supernatural Bias of Ex-Christians (and other important topics)*, the topic of the Rapture was dealt with in light of history. There is a rumor in which it is believed that a young woman named Margaret MacDonald came up with the idea in the mid-1800s. This theory was then shared with her pastor, J. N. Darby, who allegedly ran with it and created an entire doctrine surrounding it.

The chapter in my book responded to the question of the Rapture's true origin, and we were not the first to show from history that the doctrine of the Rapture occurring prior to the Tribulation period had been espoused by others *before* Margaret MacDonald. Moreover, documentation shows that it was espoused *well before* MacDonald is supposed to have visualized it. In fact, documents prove that the Rapture (though not named as such) was taught as far back as the 5th or 6th century A.D., and possibly even earlier. This then proved that the Margaret MacDonald rumor is just that; a rumor. For more information, please refer to *The Anti-Supernatural Bias of Ex-Christians*.

In today's society, there are groups who look at life, death, heaven and hell much differently than the average Christian. That has always been the case, since the birth of the Church (in Acts 2). In this day and age, though, it has become much more noticeable than in years prior.

This is at least in part due to the fact that within Christendom, there are those who deny the doctrine of the Rapture, as well as other biblical doctrines related to the End Times. However, with the influx of humanity to the United States in search of safe harbor over the past few decades, new languages, new cultures, and even new religions have come to the fore. These have in essence questioned the truth of Christianity as never before because of the beliefs they bring with them to these shores.

Couple all of this with the tremendously fast growth of technology, and it is nearly impossible for a person to sneeze in New York City without the rest of the world knowing about it seconds later. Technology has literally put us on the fast track of communication, and precious little time goes by before some piece of news is splashed across web pages on the Internet. Before long, everyone knows of it and is involved in discussions concerning it, if the news is worthy of discussion.

The world has grown to a point of no return. We cannot go back to the days *before* there were computers, cell phones, or satellite communication. All of this is here to stay, and it has its good and bad associated with it. It appears that while computers and technology were originally designed to make life easier while increasing productivity, much of what technology offers has in truth become a noose around our necks.

Walk down a street today and see how far you can travel before you find someone talking on their cell phone. Go to a library and see if you can find someone who does not have a laptop with them, hooked up to the Internet and running. Cell phones are not simply devices we use to make phone calls any longer, either. Today's cell phone takes pictures, records conversation and video, has many applications that can be downloaded to it and many even come with built in tiny keyboards allowing the owner to create and send text messages more quickly.

Video cameras, once costing thousands of dollars, are now available for less than one hundred dollars. While the quality of the video is not as good as the higher end models, of course, the low cost puts a video camera in range of just about everyone's budget. Because of this, a proliferation of TV programming focusing on spills, thrills and foibles of John Q. Citizen, crazy drivers, and stupid criminals fills our TV screens for those who care to watch.

Security cameras are everywhere. It is impossible to go into a store, a mall, even doctors' offices and the like without seeing a video camera recording your actions. Cameras are placed on certain intersections in order to catch drivers going through red lights. Where can one hide from "Big Brother's" watchful eye? While all of these cameras create a sense of security for many, they also remove certain civil rights and freedoms that this country has been known for having. Still, it seems that the majority is willing to make that trade-off to have a greater sense of safety while in public.

More and more items today are produced with computerized parts. Cars, TVs, DVD players, phones, microwave ovens, dishwashers, washers and dryers and even tools now have computerized parts and chips in them. This supposedly makes the product work better, yet they are more pricey because of that. No longer can someone just "tinker" with a product and fix something. It often requires a computer wizard and barring that, replacing the item. Except for products that have no motorized mechanisms, it is difficult to think of an item that is completely devoid of computer technology.

As mentioned, one of the interesting side effects of this type of technology is the ability to transmit and receive information much more quickly. Go to any of the online free video places where anyone can post a video and every topic under the sun can be located there. These topics extend to the full range of subjects, some that were even either completely downplayed before, or only discussed with other individuals who were of like mind in order not to be seen as loopy.

One such subject today has to do with extra-terrestrials and UFOs. Years ago, this was a very touchy subject. It just was not discussed by people who were considered to be *normal*. Once someone entered into one of these discussions and signified any type of belief at all in the UFO phenomenon, the person was seen as being a bit *abnormal* and generally avoided.

However, in the last few decades, a number of things have occurred which have made discussion of UFOs much more acceptable and even credible. No longer are we discussing *little green men* from Mars. People routinely discuss the different species of extra-terrestrial life forms that supposedly have visited, or even *routinely* visit, from beyond our solar system.

In the 1970s, this entire area of discussion really took off and not just by people of whom others would think to be a bit off in their heads. NASA astronauts, think tanks, intellectuals, talk show hosts, commercial airline pilots and many more began including dialogue about intelligent life forms outside of our solar system as being viable and real, and they have gone on to state that contact has been made.

Go on the Internet today and it is not at all difficult to find information about the various species of ETs with simply a few search words, followed by a few clicks. There are essentially six alien species that are "known" by people in the world today:

- *Raelians*
- *Pleadians*
- *Greys*
- *Reptilians*
- *Insectoids*
- *Venusians*

What is even more interesting than simply reading the names of these supposed species is *what* they allegedly attempt to accomplish with humans on this planet. The Raelians are said to be beings which are reptile-looking in nature. These are the ones who it is believed do most of the human abductions. While in their captivity, humans are examined and messages are given to the individual from the Raelians via a form of mental telepathy.

Apparently, not much is known about the Pleadians, but the Greys are the ones that we see in drawings, TV programs and movies most often. The movie *Close Encounters of the Third Kind* portrayed this type of alien.

Reptilians are half-human, half-reptile and Insectoids supposedly look like the lovable alien in the movie *ET*. Venusians are beings said to be from the planet Venus. TV shows and a plethora of Sci-Fi movies related to the UFO genre have made it much easier to digest and discuss aspects of what has become known as Ufology.

Now, while it is easy to read this and roll the eyes, the most interesting part of this breaks down into two aspects:

1. *The people who believe these beings exist really believe these beings exist, and these folks are from all walks of life.*
2. *The message that is consistently given by these alien life forms is one of a religious nature.*

If number one did not get your attention, number two should have. If you go to any of the websites on the Internet related to aliens, UFOs and ETs (along with other unexplained phenomena), you can read for yourself many of the stories and narratives that have been reported. Beyond this, there are snapshots of photos purportedly highlighting some type of UFO craft. Videos can often be found as well. Certainly, some of these are faked (but very good fakes), but there are some that even the experts have not been able to legitimately dismiss, so the jury is still out.

If time is taken to talk personally with these individuals (I have not) or read articles which contain interviews with some of these people, it becomes obvious that these people cannot be merely dismissed out of hand. They are sincere, they are intelligent and they firmly believe that they have had some type of experience (if they were abducted by aliens).

There have been many books published on the topic of alien abductions or things related to aliens. Many seem to be published by people that might be called "crackpots," or those simply hoping to make a fast buck. Other publications are not so easy to ignore, while still others have a good deal of believability to them.

One such book is published by Koinonia House and is co-written by Chuck Missler and Mark Eastman. They have a good deal to say about the possibilities behind this burgeoning alien trend.

There has been documented (some with video) evidence of huge UFO events over the past three to four decades. A number of these videos are easily found on the Internet. The event of January 1, 1993 in Mexico City is one such occurrence. It was reported that on that day, *"a silvery craft [was seen by thousands] performing aerial acrobatics over the central portion of Mexico City in broad daylight."*[17]

UFOs Abound

Missler indicates that later the same day, other craft arrived to join the first one. Again, in this particular instance, thousands of people saw the event and many recorded it. Since the early 90s, UFO sightings have increased tremendously. It is almost as if the aliens (if they actually exist) *want* to be noticed.

In 1996, over Israel, there occurred another bold UFO sighting. Apparently, this particular UFO simply hovered near the city of Tel Aviv for a while, then began doing tremendous aerial acrobatics. The

---

[17] Chuck Missler, *Alien Encounters* (Coeur d'Alene: Koinonia House 1997), 12

speed and dexterity with which this object was able to accomplish this cannot apparently be replicated by any known technology today.

As we continue on through the 90s, we see more and more eye-witness accounts of UFOs appearing in the sky in various parts of the world. Beyond this, there has also been a huge upsurge in alien abduction claims. Missler's book lists many of these incidents and the reader is encouraged to avail themselves of not only Chuck's book, but also other books that provide additional corroboration.

In my opinion, these beings may in fact be spirit beings we often refer to as *demons*, who, as part of a growing worldwide deception, are disguising themselves as aliens from other worlds. Many of the so-called messages that abductees have received from them are nearly the same and they almost always include the sense that these aliens want nothing more than to *help* us and our world. This has become the standard tune of these beings, as reported by countless abductees.

It appears that in their desire to help us, these aliens also come to us with a *warning* – a warning that if not heeded, would mean earth's ultimate demise. In some ways, of course, this sounds overly dramatic, and very much like an episode of *Star Trek*, or *Star Wars*, or some other sci-fi program of similar nature. The problem though is that this is *not* a TV program or movie. The situation as understood or seen by many people appears *real* in nature, and that reality continues to grow as that global group of abductees becomes larger as time goes by.

So according to many people who say they have been abducted, examined, poked, prodded and given messages (telepathically), the underlying communication to the citizens of earth is that these aliens are coming to visit us more and more because of their concern for our welfare. They are anxious because they do not want us to destroy ourselves. They are worried because they also want to ensure that we get to the next *evolutionary* level. This is what they *say* through transmitted messages to us, from their brain to ours. Here then is where it becomes interesting.

Missler clarifies for us. *"One might expect that such a visitation from our "space parents" would be accompanied by detailed information on how to solve our increasing global difficulties. With their supposed highly advanced technology, surely they would have solved the kinds of political, economic, environmental, and medical problems we now face. And yet, no such message [has been] given. Instead, Rael [a person so-named by the visiting aliens – ed.] was given a religious message – in effect, a Bible study conducted by an ET!"*[18]

What Is Their Message?
That is interesting, isn't it? Here we are on earth, with poverty-stricken nations, disease running rampant, seemingly insurmountable economic difficulties, and no cure for cancer, AIDS, or the common cold, yet these aliens seem not to have anything to offer about those things. Instead they are intent upon explaining the *real* meaning of the Bible to at least some of the abductees.

Missler continues; *"The primary message that the extraterrestrials wanted Rael to understand was that they created mankind. According to Rael, the extraterrestrials told him that they created humanity in their image by sophisticated genetic engineering techniques."*[19] Rael continues in his book titled *The Message Given to Me by Extraterrestrials* by explaining and describing the *actual* story of Creation, not the one most of us have read and know found in the first few chapters of Genesis.

If all this is not interesting enough, we find that another one of the main messages being given to earthlings by aliens is one which might cause fear in many at first glance. This message, if not for the fact that it has been distilled through several individuals on earth at various

---

[18] Chuck Missler, *Alien Encounters* (Coeur d'Alene: Koinonia House 1997), 136
[19] Ibid

times, would be extremely difficult to believe. Yet here is a message given by ETs and recorded in *The Ashtar Command, Project World Evacuation, 1993*: *"Our rescue ships will be able to come in close enough in the twinkling of an eye to set the lifting beams in operation in a moment. And all over the globe where events warrant it, this will be the method of evacuation. Mankind will be lifted, levitated shall we say, by the beams from our smaller ships. These smaller craft will in turn taxi the persons to the larger ships overhead, higher in the atmosphere, where there is ample space and quarters and supplies for millions of people."*[20]

What was that?! Did they say an *evacuation* of "millions of people"? These series of Ashtar Command messages transmitted to a person named *Tuella* are on the Internet and can be easily read by simply searching the 'Net. The entire book starts out with this small disclaimer: *"Although these Messages of the coming Earth Changes and Ascension of Planet Earth given by the Ashtar Command in the 1980's through Tuella (Thelma Terrell) have since been long delayed in their outcome,* **mainly through the strong efforts of the Forces of Darkness to eliminate or postpone the event***, the instruction and program contained therein remains largely unchanged and applicable to the now fast approaching times of final cleansing."*[21] (emphasis added)

Notice what is being stated here. Apparently, these messages were originally transmitted in the 1980s. It was thought then (by the "aliens") that what they were stating was going to come to pass *soon*. It did not, so this disclaimer was placed as an excuse. The average individual, however, will look at this and say *"See? It's the Forces of Darkness that are working against world peace! We've got to work harder!"*

---

[20] Chuck Missler, *Alien Encounters* (Coeur d'Alene: 1997), 187
[21] Ibid

According to Missler, the first messages from the Ashtar Command arrived in 1952 to author George Van Tassel. *"We are concerned about [humanity's] deliberate determination to EXTINGUISH HUMANITY AND TURN THIS PLANET INTO A CINDER...Our missions are peaceful, but this condition occurred before in this solar system and the planet Lucifer was torn to bits. We are determined that it shall not happen again."*[22]

What is engrossing here is that if we compare this with the biblical picture, we gain some insight into what these beings know. In spite of the fact that many within Christendom do not believe in the doctrine of the Rapture, here is a *type* of Rapture being postulated by aliens!

1) The fact that these aliens have already sent messages about a coming evacuation of millions of people from this planet is obviously their attempt to downplay the biblical Rapture. The Rapture according to the Bible is the instantaneous *translation* of authentic Christians, who make up the invisible Church. This will happen in a moment, in the twinkling of an eye. Paul speaks of this event in 1 Thessalonians 4:15-17: *"...the Lord himself will descend from heaven with a cry of command, with the voice of an archangel, and with the sound of the trumpet of God. And the dead in Christ will rise first. Then we who are alive, who are left, will be caught up together with them in the clouds to meet the Lord in the air, and so we will always be with the Lord."* This is also reflected in Christ's own Olivet Discourse found in Matthew 24:29-31.

Here we see in a message purportedly transmitted *by* an alien from the Ashtar Command *to* a human being that these aliens have been preparing the earth for a time in which millions of people would vanish instantly from the face of the earth.

Thelma Terrell (or Tuela as she is known in New Age circles) carried on where Van Tassel left off. *"In the 1980s Ashtar clarified the message*

---

[22] Barbara Marciniak, *Bringers of the Dawn*

to Earth through a new channeler named Thelma Terrell...she compiled the channeled messages of Ashtar, who declared that planet Earth would be spared certain annihilation by an extraterrestrial evacuation of millions of people who **threaten the harmony and evolution of Earth** *(emphasis added)."*[23]

Ah, so it becomes *clearer*. First we learn that the aliens have transmitted messages as early as 1952 which tell of a removal of millions of people from the earth, all in the same instant. Then in the 1980s, another person by the name of Tuela, who has apparently replaced the deceased Van Tassel, received clarified information from this same source that the people who are to be removed are those that *threaten earth's existence.*

What is fascinating of course is that all of this sounds like the Rapture to me. It is a fact that Satan knows the Bible and he likely knows it better than any other living human being (besides Christ Himself). During Christ's temptation in the wilderness, Satan quoted Scripture – the Word of God – just as he had in the Garden of Eden. He quoted it in the same manner, slightly twisting the meaning of it, so that while it *resembled* its original meaning, it now meant something else.

Jesus did not buy any of it, rejecting Satan's advances with Scripture of His own. Satan's deceptive ploys were not strong enough to remove Jesus off the chosen path. The reader is encouraged to read this narrative of Jesus' bout with Satan, and His victory of the same (Matthew 4, Mark 1, and Luke 4).

Satan Knows the Rapture *Will* Occur

Are the powers of Darkness, led by Satan himself, fully aware of an event that Paul speaks of in which all true believers (both dead and alive at the time) will be *caught up*, to be forever with the Lord? It would appear so, but notice that in Satan's version of this event, those

---

[23] http://www.share-international.org/background/bcreme/bc_main.htm 06/05/2009

who are "raptured" or evacuated off the planet are the *problem* children. It is these folks who are keeping the *rest* of the population and the world itself from evolving into the next stage of existence.

It is not merely Chuck Missler and Mark Eastman that provide us with information that seems to indicate a Rapture-like event of the true Church will occur in the future. Others like Constance Cumby have also written about the New Age Movement, critiquing the new world order that New Agers long for and look forward to becoming a reality. This new world order may very well include aspects of Neo-Nazism, along with solid components of the New Age Movement, which is sadly already finding its way into many mainline churches and denominations.

Referring to this possible future event Christians call the Rapture, one New Age writer states this: *"The people who leave the planet during the time of Earth changes do not fit in here any longer, and they are stopping the harmony of Earth. When the time comes that perhaps 20 million people leave the planet at one time there will be a tremendous shift in consciousness for those who are remaining."*[24]

On the Share International website, Benjamin Crème is noted as *"a messenger of hope."*[25] He is called this due to his connection with the spirit world and his ability to channel the "Masters," which have ultimately become known to Crème as the Hierarchy of the Masters.

In the late 1950s, after having spent a number of years studying the writings of Blavatsky, Alice Bailey and others, Crème began receiving what he called transmissions from these Masters. The first of these transmissions informed Crème of an eventual appearance of Maitreya,

---

[24] http://www.share-international.org/background/bcreme/bc_main.htm 06/05/2009
[25] http://www.share-international.org

or the Christ, whom Crème referred to as *"Head of our planetary Hierarchy."*[26]

Between the years of 1959 and 1974, the transmissions occurred with some regularity, and Crème became deep friends with the one he called simply *the Master*. This individual taught Crème things about life, reincarnation, the hierarchy, the higher consciousness and everything connected with the New Age Movement, and the coming new world order that he had *not* learned through the writings of Blavatsky and Bailey.

Not long afterward, Crème began having meetings with others of like mind to introduce them to the world of the New Age Movement and the coming changes that would occur on this planet. A few years after he began these meetings he received another transmission, but instead of it coming from his Master, this one apparently came directly from Maitreya himself. Crème relates this event: *"In June 1974 began a series of overshadowing and transmitted messages by Maitreya, inspiring us, and keeping us informed of the progress of his externalisation. We were privileged also to become aware of the gradual creation and perfectionment of his body of manifestation — the Mayavirupa. In the period from March 1976 to September 1977, these communications from Maitreya became very frequent indeed."*[27]

This was not to be the only message from Maitreya either. There were many more: *"Between September 1977 and June 1982, British author and lecturer Benjamin Crème received a series of 140 Messages from Maitreya, the World Teacher."*[28]

In message number 140, transmitted in May of 1982, Maitreya stated this (in part) through Crème: *"It has been My intention to reveal Myself at the earliest possible moment, to brook no delay, and to come*

---

[26] http://www.share-international.org/background/bcreme/bc_main.htm 06/05/2009
[27] Ibid
[28] Ibid

before the world as your Friend and Teacher. Much depends on My immediate discovery, for in this way can I help you to save your world. I am here to aid and teach, to show you the path to the future, and to reveal you to each other as Gods."[29]

One of the questions that must be asked is twofold: what is keeping the future evacuation from occurring and what is stopping Maitreya from making himself known to the world? In reality, there is only one thing that keeps these events from unfolding.

Satan is *not* all-knowing, or all-powerful. He cannot be in more than one place at the same time. Apart from all these things, he does *not* know every detail about the future. He only knows what he sees in the Bible. As I have stated in another book I have written (*Dispensationalism's View of God's Sovereignty*), this is one of the largest reasons why God has chosen to have *progressively* revealed His will to humanity. The more God revealed to humanity, the more Satan knew, so God kept many things close to His chest, so to speak. He only revealed things as He saw fit and only what mankind needed to know at that moment. Yes, man was in the dark about any number of things, but so was Satan.

Satan Reads the Bible
Because Satan only knows what he learns through the revelation of Scripture, along with what he sees God actually doing, he does not know the day or the hour of many events which are said to be connected to the End Times. If the Rapture is slated to occur, as we believe the Bible teaches it will, no one knows exactly *when* that event will occur. The exact day and hour is not listed in Scripture. The closest we get to it is when Jesus speaks of the times nearing the Great Tribulation in Matthew 24 (see also Mark 13 and Luke 21). He speaks of the fact that His disciples knew when the seasons were changing by looking at the trees. It is by that change that we know

---

[29] http://www.share-international.org/background/bcreme/bc_main.htm 06/05/2009

one season blends into another. In the same way, Christ gave us clues or signs to look for which would signal the *beginning* of the end.

As Fruchtenbaum states in *Footsteps of the Messiah,* as far as the Jewish rabbis of old were concerned, there were simply two ages; this age and the age to come. In Matthew 24, when Christ speaks of the end of the age, He is referring to the end of *this* age, which is controlled by *man's rule* (but of course, overseen by God). This age will end when Jesus returns physically to set up His kingdom on earth and will also physically rule from David's throne in Jerusalem. This is what separates this age from the next: Christ's return.

The signs Jesus spoke of in the Olivet Discourse were given to serve as a way to keep track of and to watch for things as this age began to wind down. Much speculation, argumentation and debate about what Jesus meant has raged on. Within the past few decades, the belief that most prophetic events have already occurred in the past, leaving only a few chapters in the last part of Revelation to occur, has gained momentum. This is at least part of the reason I included this chapter: because the modern trend in much of the visible Church believes that Christ's return, far from being the physical return that the two "men" in Acts 1 pointed to, was *spiritual* in nature and occurred in A.D. 70 with the destruction of Jerusalem and the Temple.

This belief seems to stem from Scripture, but in truth, what many Christians today are advocating is a *gradual improvement* in society. Once we wipe out famine, disease and the like, man himself will be much improved. This improvement will by itself usher in a new form of spiritual Christianity, one in which Christ as the absolute head of the Church will be able to reign from heaven through *all* creatures on earth. Unfortunately, as stated, this is in marked contrast with what the Bible teaches and the literal meaning that stems from that teaching.

In his book *Satan: His Motives and Methods*, Lewis Sperry Chafer pointed out then (in 1919) that a belief in a spiritual form of fulfillment had taken place by Christ. This of course was at odds with the orthodox evangelical position, which looked to the yet future physical return of Jesus. Chafer has this to say regarding this modern belief: *"Well may believers study their own motives in service in view of these vastly differing programs; and question whether there is in them a humble willingness to cooperate in the present purpose of God in preparing the Bride for the returning King. Or whether, on the other hand, they have carelessly fallen in with the Satanic ideal which rejects the coming kingdom of Christ by an unholy attempt to establish the present kingdom of Satan."*[30]

So on one hand, we see humanity – including many within the visible Church – catering to the ideas presented by the enemy that if we all work hard enough, we will one day attain that which we long for in Christ. It is unfortunate that these people are blinded to the truth of the Bible, with its plain, clear message of future events.

Those who receive the message of His Word plainly, understanding its meaning in literal terms, look for the signs that Christ spoke of in His Olivet Discourse. While these signs do not necessarily pinpoint the exact timing of future events, they let us know whether or not the beginning of birth pains has already begun, or is yet future. We see these signs as simply that: *indicators* allowing us to see the progression of things to their chosen culmination.

Satan does the same thing. Through his demonic horde, he keeps abreast of what is going on throughout the world and attempts to judge the times and seasons, but that is the best he can do. He does not know when the Rapture will occur, and for that matter does not know when many other events will occur which are related to the End Times. This is why he constantly has to "correct" or "clarify"

---

[30] Lewis Sperry Chafer, *Satan His Motives and Methods* (Grand Rapids: Kregal 1990), 67-68

things through his messengers as time moves onward, leaving unfulfilled the things he transmitted years before to unknowing and deceived human beings.

What we know is that the New Age Movement believes that one day, due to "ignorance" and "an inability to evolve," millions of people will be suddenly and instantly removed from the face of this planet. Satan has made preparation for this upcoming event by announcing it ahead of time, but simply putting a completely different twist on it.

If the event simply occurred, with absolutely no notice given to humanity, it is likely that at least some people would remember being taught about it from the Bible. They would panic, realizing that the Bible prophecy concerning the Rapture had actually occurred! They *were,* in point of fact, left behind.

This would not work for Satan's plan at all. He would have to do something to draw attention away from the fact that this concept is taught in Scripture. He has a number of choices at his disposal, both of which he seems to have done:

1. **For Christians (professing and true)**: Create doubt within them, so that they themselves do not believe the Rapture will occur. Have them focus on the rumor that Margaret MacDonald actually created the concept. If there are Christians who literally deny that the Rapture is going to occur, then this is what they will teach to everyone, those who believe it and those who do not believe it.
2. **For the Non-Christians (New Agers)**: Get the word out way ahead of time that the Rapture *will* occur; however, the Bible has it wrong. The Great Evacuation will occur to remove Christians from the world, but as far as the world will understand it, these Christians are seen as trouble makers, keeping the planet and people from evolving to the next level.

Certainly, this is one reason why Satan began to disseminate his own version of the event of the Rapture. He *knows* without doubt that it *will* take place, unlike many Christians today, who deny a good deal of the as-yet-unfulfilled prophetic discourse. Some Christians, to be sure, are not in rebellion to God, nor do they desire to work against Him, but they are blind to His purposes related to the End Times. It is because of this that they *do* wind up inadvertently working against Him and His purposes. They do not envision a coming Rapture and many do not envision a coming Great Tribulation either, having sequestered the latter to the A.D. 70 event of Jerusalem's destruction.

Satan, on the other hand, knows the Rapture will occur. He knows the Great Tribulation will occur and it is for this event that he is directing much of his energy and power. It is during this time that Satan will reveal himself to the world through the Antichrist as a kind, intelligent, loving, tolerant man who because of these things will rise to rule the entire world through a global government of *Absolute Imperialism.*

Though Satan is working toward the final showdown that will occur at the end of the Great Tribulation, he does not know *when* either the Rapture or the Great Tribulation will actually occur. These times are in God's hands only, and only when that time arrives will the Rapture of the Church occur. After that, the beginning of the Great Tribulation (comprising a full seven years) will start, when the Antichrist is able to gain the trust of Israel, entering into a covenant with her for the seven years of the Tribulation/Great Tribulation.

Ever watchful, Satan continues to keep tabs on everything that happens in this world that he has no control over. This allows him to judge the times and seasons, but as we have seen, though that is not enough, it is the best he can do.

The Rapture According to Satan

"professing themselves wise, they became as fools" Romans 1:22

FOR NEW AGERS:
People are being told that sometime in the future, an evacuation of millions of people will occur in the "twinkling of an eye." These people are said to keep the planet and its citizenry from evolving to the next level. Their removal means progression for the planet.

"scoffers will come in the last days" 2 Peter 3:3

FOR DOUBTERS:
These folks believe rumors like Margaret MacDonald started the Rapture story and Darby ran with it. Others believe that the Rapture was created by people who are merely looking for a persecution escape clause, or a fast way to make a quick buck.

Even when things are clarified by Maitreya or some other entity as to why, for instance, the great planetary evacuation has not yet taken place, or why Maitreya himself has been unable to reveal himself, the blame is placed on those with *bad energy*. Because these things are happening as spoken of through theses transmissions given over the space of twenty or thirty years, it is stated or implied that those who *keep things* from happening are the problem people of this world. So instead of doubting Maitreya's power and ability, eyes turn to the *problem* to see what can be done about that.

Within the New Age Movement, the concept of *energy* – both positive and negative – is *foundational*. Those having a positive energy are enabled to move things forward to the next evolutionary phase. Those with a negative energy (read: *Christians*) keep things *from* happening the way the New Age adherents have been told it is scheduled to happen.

One day, as has been noted, according to New Age beliefs, space ships will park themselves above our skies, out of sight. Then, at the appointed time, they will literally *vacuum* the earth of that which keeps the planet and the people on it from entering a new phase of reality. Thus, the problem of earth's inability to rise to the next level of evolution will have been dealt with once and for all. Nothing then would continue to stand in the way of earth's advancement.

What is to be done with all these millions of people who are instantly whisked away from the planet? We look again to Chuck Missler, who quotes from the spring 1994 issue of *Connecting Link Magazine* from an article written by Kay Wheeler. Wheeler provides clarification on this upcoming event when millions in an instant will wind up missing. She states, "*Many of these beings who are leaving this planet at this time have completed that which they came to do. It is a time of great rejoicing for them. Do not feel sad about their leaving. They are going home. Many are waiting to be with them again...Many beings must move on, for their thought patterns are of the past. They hold on to these thoughts that keep Earth held back."*[31] Notice how Wheeler has *softened* the blow a bit here. While she states that these individuals are holding the Earth back from its natural evolutionary advancement, she states that these humans (referred to as "beings") are going to a better place, so while the world should experience a collective sigh of relief, it should also revel in the fact that these missing people are going to a better place.

I find that especially interesting, because what Wheeler is describing is exactly what the Christian longs for as they look to Christ for the fulfillment of it. In looking closely at what Wheeler has stated, there is a good deal of truth in it; however, the beings that have revealed this information to Wheeler want her to understand *not* that the people Raptured off the planet are going to be with Jesus. He is not even mentioned at all. They want her to understand that this future event is all part of their specific evolutionary path, a path in which they will:

1. *Rejoice*
2. *Go home*
3. *Be reunited with loved ones*

This is the perfect picture of what the Christian will experience once this life is left behind. We know that Satan is a liar and the hordes of demons lie as he lies, taking their cue from him. To mix truth with their lies is what comes naturally to them, and if it brings about their chosen ends, all the better.

Satan goes on the offensive where the Rapture is concerned. Those within the church who deny that the Rapture is a biblical doctrine have obviously not been paying attention. While they are arguing over meaning of passages of Scripture, they have missed a very large indicator that the Bible is true. Satan and his cohorts have been

---

[31] Chuck Missler, *Alien Encounters* (Coeur d'Alene: Koinonia House 1997), 189

telling those lost individuals who have become firmly established in the New Age Movement that such an event *will* occur. They have, however, given it their own special meaning.

The question then regarding the possibility of the Rapture is simply this: if the Rapture was/is truly a doctrine of devils with absolutely no biblical basis, as some charge, then what possible reason would Satan have in creating any kind of deception surrounding it? If it is not in danger of taking place at all, why would he bother with it? It would be one thing to create that false teaching simply to confuse Christians and get them arguing with one another. It is quite another thing altogether to teach *non-believers* the concept of a Rapture-like event that will occur in the future.

To create a scenario with this amount of detail, related to what *will* happen (but won't) when the Rapture takes place, so that it is seen as something else entirely, would not only be counter-productive to his goals and purposes, but worse than that, makes him appear as someone who really has no clue about what is happening, if the Rapture was not going to actually occur. Certainly, he would not directly be affected negatively, but his plan would, and those through whom he is working and speaking would immediately lose all of their credibility. It simply makes absolutely no sense for Satan to create such a charade based around an event that is *not* in the least biblical. On the other hand, if the Rapture *is* slated to occur as the Bible teaches, then Satan has a very good reason for trying to create a diversion by teaching that what is happening is not a biblical event, but one that has to do with the earth's advancement on the evolutionary timeline.

The Rapture is a biblical event. It is clear not only from Scripture, but from what the enemy of our souls is telling those who are caught in the web of his lies and deceit. The last thing Satan wants the average, unsaved person to know is the *truth* concerning the Rapture. That will not do at all. Better they see this upcoming event as something

The Rapture and the Second Coming

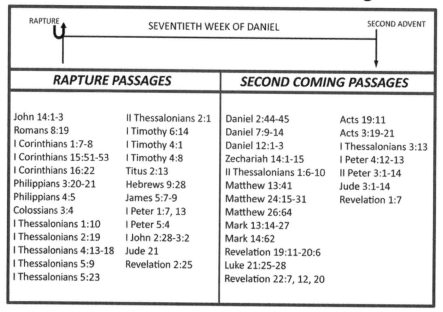

RAPTURE PASSAGES		SECOND COMING PASSAGES	
John 14:1-3	II Thessalonians 2:1	Daniel 2:44-45	Acts 19:11
Romans 8:19	I Timothy 6:14	Daniel 7:9-14	Acts 3:19-21
I Corinthians 1:7-8	I Timothy 4:1	Daniel 12:1-3	I Thessalonians 3:13
I Corinthians 15:51-53	I Timothy 4:8	Zechariah 14:1-15	I Peter 4:12-13
I Corinthians 16:22	Titus 2:13	II Thessalonians 1:6-10	II Peter 3:1-14
Philippians 3:20-21	Hebrews 9:28	Matthew 13:41	Jude 3:1-14
Philippians 4:5	James 5:7-9	Matthew 24:15-31	Revelation 1:7
Colossians 3:4	I Peter 1:7, 13	Matthew 26:64	
I Thessalonians 1:10	I Peter 5:4	Mark 13:14-27	
I Thessalonians 2:19	I John 2:28-3:2	Mark 14:62	
I Thessalonians 4:13-18	Jude 21	Revelation 19:11-20:6	
I Thessalonians 5:9	Revelation 2:25	Luke 21:25-28	
I Thessalonians 5:23		Revelation 22:7, 12, 20	

15 Contrasting Events of the Second Coming

RAPTURE/BLESSED HOPE	GLORIOUS APPEARING
1) Christ comes in air for His own	1) Christ comes with His own to earth
2) Rapture/translation of all Christians	2) No one translated
3) Christians taken to Father's House	3) Resurrected saints do not see Father's House
4) No judgment on earth at Rapture	4) Christ judges inhabitants of earth
5) Church taken to Heaven at Rapture	5) Christ sets up His kingdom on earth
6) Rapture imminent	6) Glorious appearing cannot occur for 7 years
7) No signs for the Rapture	7) Many signs for Christ's physical coming
8) For believers only	8) Affects all humanity
9) Time of joy	9) Time of mourning
10) Before the Day of Wrath (Tribulation)	10) Immediately after Tribulation (Matthew 24)
11) No mention of Satan	11) Satan bound in Abyss for 1,000 years
12) The Judgment Seat of Christ	12) No time or place for Judgment Seat
13) Marriage of the Lamb	13) His bride descends with Him
14) Only His own see Him	14) Every eye will see Him
15) Tribulation can begin	15) 1,000-year kingdom of Christ begins

he designed (through those appearing as aliens) for the good of this planet and the good of humanity. He gains much by also having *Christians* come to disbelieve in the veracity of the Rapture doctrine.

The charts on the previous page highlight passages referring to the Rapture and Second Coming (culled from Fruchtenbaum's book *Footsteps of the Messiah*). The top chart compares passages of Scripture connected with the Second Coming to those connected with the Rapture. The bottom chart compares and contrasts the events themselves and as can be seen, there are many differences between these two events.

The charts were created by the author and are based on information from the book by Dr. Arnold G. Fruchtenbaum, *The Footsteps of the Messiah*. The reader is encouraged to study the various sections of Scripture listed in each to determine just exactly what these differences are between the two events. Beyond this, for a complete detailing of these two events, the aforementioned book by Dr. Fruchtenbaum is a must for anyone's library.

The chart on the next page (also based on information provided in Fruchtenbaum's book *Footsteps of the Messiah*) outlines the *Promise of the Rapture*, the *Program of the Rapture* and the *Timing of the Rapture*. The clear teaching of Scripture designates a specific event in which all in Christ (the Church) are translated, or *caught up* to be with Him in the clouds. This event, unlike the Second Coming, is *not* a return of Christ to earth. In this event, He merely steps away from His throne, out of the third heaven, and *greets* His Bride as His Bride is translated.

This event is also very similar to the way Enoch was *translated* prior to the judgment of the global flood in Genesis 4. Enoch walked with God and *"was not because the Lord took him."* Enoch, then, was removed from this earth alive. He did *not* see death. This is the exact sense in which Christ's Bride, having already been purified due to His

shed blood on Calvary's cross, is caught up to be with Him forever. Many people today teach that the Church needs to be purified before we are able to be presented to Him blameless. This is a false teaching. Paul teaches that there is therefore _now_ NO condemnation to those who are in Christ Jesus (Romans 8:1). For the Christian, there should be no fear in standing before Jesus Christ in judgment (for our salvation).

The Church awaits the *fullness of the Gentiles* (cf. Romans 11), which is the time we are now living in. During this phase, God continues to call out those earmarked for salvation from every nation and culture. When the last of these has been called out, the fullness of the Gentiles will have been reached. The reader is encouraged to read through the passages highlighted in the charts seen on the previous pages.

In a day and age when people are balking at the doctrine of Jesus' return, it is important to honestly understand what the Bible teaches. Is the Rapture grounded doctrinally in His Word, or is it a figment of someone's overworked imagination? Because of what the New Age is teaching throughout its loose knit network of adherents, it would appear that Satan knows the Rapture will occur. It is because of this that he has taken the time to thoroughly indoctrinate his followers with the truth of the Rapture, but with his own special twist, via the teachings of aliens. It certainly seems to be working.

Christians should spend at least some time determining what is being taught within the New Age. After all, this is where Satan lies to his own followers, yet he does so by mixing the truth of Scripture with his own falsehoods. The New Age movement is nothing but the continuation of the system of Babylon, officially begun by Nimrod in Genesis 11. It was there that Satan made a grab to unite all of humanity under one banner.

While God thwarted Satan's efforts then, he (Satan) has worked continually to reestablish what was lost at the Tower of Babel. Today, thousands of years later, Satan has once again nearly created a society where people are one in thought, word, and deed. The only ones who are left out of the picture (by choice) are authentic Christians. There is no room for authentic Christians in the New Age movement since the teachings of that movement are diametrically opposed to God.

All the teachings of the New Age through aliens, ascended masters, or anyone else can be summed up in one statement: *you shall be as gods*. It doesn't matter how varied the message is, because it always comes down to the same thought. Often, the message is wrapped in Christian-sounding terms, as we have noted. On other occasions, it seems to be completely separate from God or religion, yet a religious flavor remains.

Many examples of transmitted messages from entities beyond our range of sight offer up ethereal platitudes that draw people into an ever widening web of lies. This is often done by including verbiage from Scripture and simply providing a different context for it. Thus, the lie is created simply because of the *context* in which it is placed and very little of the wording needs to be changed. This has become clear with transmissions from Kay Wheeler, Barbara Marciniak, Benhamin Crème, and others who use phrases that are cleverly disguised to sound authentically biblical (to convince those who are somewhat familiar with the Bible). In the end, though, the messages are nothing more than lies because of their context.

Whether the message is provided to us by Kay Wheeler, Barbara Marciniak, or someone else entirely, the messages serve to alleviate the tremendous amount of stress that the average person will experience when the Rapture does occur.

Consider that when the Rapture happens, millions of lives will be affected. People driving cars, flying airplanes, and doing a million and one other things will be gone in the twinkling of an eye. Think of the chaos that will result for those left on the earth after this event. Think of how traumatic this will be for this planet.

On one hand, New Agers will delight in the idea that the malcontents are gone. Once the cleanup starts, the real process of advancing to the next spiritual plane can begin. Those who are taken completely off guard will need quite a bit of reassurance by those who are "in the know" of the New Age movement.

Don't you find it alarming, if not fascinating, that Satan has spent so much time indoctrinating those within the New Age that the Rapture will occur? Though he has given it a new name – *Great Evacuation* – it is clearly the Rapture that is being taught.

When the Rapture *does* occur, the only people who will be surprised are those not involved in the New Age at all. However, New Agers will be on hand to explain the event in New Age terminology in an attempt to ease the fears of those left behind.

The Rapture will cause a great amount of excitement in the hearts of New Agers left standing when the dust settles. Think of it. This one event will be the greatest signal to adherents of the New Age that things are ramping up to complete the next evolutionary jump to the next spiritual plane.

Once the Church is gone, a tremendous hole will be left, and that hole will quickly be filled with Satan's energies. When the Church is taken up, the Holy Spirit will not have the same direct connection with this earth that He did prior. This does not mean that God is gone from this earth. It merely means that the main vehicle through which He worked to call the unsaved of this world is no longer on the earth. This absence will immediately be filled in with a tremendous surge of satanic energy and presence. Paul is clear about this in his second letter to the Thessalonians. He states, *"For the mystery of iniquity doth already work: only he who now letteth will let, until he be taken out of the way. And then shall that Wicked be revealed, whom the Lord shall consume with the spirit of his mouth, and shall destroy with the brightness of his coming"* (2 Thessalonians 2:7-8).

Imagine a world without Christians. While some may be cheering, the stark reality will be exceedingly dangerous for this world. The presence of the Church (and the Holy Spirit through the Church) has kept evil at bay to a large extent. Without the Church, evil will be allowed to run rampant. I cannot imagine just how bad things will get and just how quickly they will occur.

It will literally become hell on earth, and yet for the most part, the people on this planet will see it as a *good* thing. This is at least what they will be told. Unfortunately, their fear will find them out and many will die because of the frightening events occurring on this planet at that time (cf. Luke 21:26; see also Revelation 6:15-17).

What about you? Where do you stand in all of this? Sitting on the fence is not an option because there is no fence to sit on. You are either on God's side or your own side. If on God's, then He will protect you. If on your own side, you are virtually on Satan's side and he will use you for his own ends. What about you?

15

Restoring What Was Lost

Whatever happens in the future will happen because God has decreed it. Satan has spent centuries working to restore what he lost at the Tower of Babel. Though severely hampered, God has allowed Satan to gather himself once again and to recreate what he once had through Nimrod.

Satan will have one more shot at usurping God and he will use his own son – the Antichrist – in his last attempt to accomplish that goal. Satan has been working so diligently to create a web of lies so convoluted and multi-faceted that it has become difficult if not impossible for the average person to connect the dots.

ALIENology

In the 1940s, the idea that aliens existed outside a radio or movie studio was absurd. You want to be fitted with a rubber jacket? Then talk about aliens in a serious tone. It just did not come across as credible.

Over the years, Satan has gained a tremendous foothold in society and advantage over the average person because of the growing acceptance of alien existence. People who were once afraid of the concept of alien races now welcome the idea with open arms.

People who believed that aliens were only the stuff of Sci-Fi books and comics now routinely discuss aspects of alien existence and communication with humans as normal. Something has changed and that something is leading this world to a new level of understanding.

Once the time has arrived, Satan will step out onto the stage of humanity through his own son, the Antichrist. During that time, one can only imagine the level of alien activity that will exist *then*.

Jesus said in His Olivet Discourse that there will be strange signs in the heavens toward the end. Aside from the physical and natural disturbances this world experiences daily through tornadoes, earthquakes, floods, and more, could He have also been alluding to a coming alien mobilization? Of course, these aliens are nothing more than demons who have neatly disguised themselves as something the world will welcome in the form of many alien races.

I believe that the reason the study of aliens is on the rise today is due solely to the fact that God has allowed Satan to have more of a global impact on society today in preparation for the revelation of the final man of sin. Things are without doubt ramping up to a level never before experienced.

Aliens are coming of age. People are intrigued and even excited about the prospect of making contact with beings believed to be far superior to us. What is not being realized, of course, is that the can of worms that will be opening up will be impossible to close. What Satan managed to take away from Adam and Eve in the Garden of Eden was the title deed to the earth. He will successfully engage in an even greater coup in the future when he manages to bring his forces to earth in the form of "aliens."

At that point in time, Satan will literally rule this earth, though only for a short period of time. He will have successfully conquered and will dominate the very earth that he stole from Adam and Eve thousands of years ago.

When Nimrod lived, Satan tried unsuccessfully to rule the earth *then*. What good is having the title deed to the earth if it was not possible to actually and physically *rule* it? Though Paul tells us that Satan is the ruler of *principalities* and ruler of the *air* (cf. Ephesians 6:12), he has yet to actually physically rule over the denizens of the earth.

This is what he has been attempting to accomplish since the Garden of Eden. However, God has thwarted him every step of the way, never allowing him to become the actual direct ruler of earth. This will change under the final stages of God's plan of redemption. Satan will be given, for a short time, his chance to rule over God's Creation.

Had Satan simply stepped out of his dimension into ours, proclaiming himself to be king of the world, how would that have gone over? Certainly, to those who worship him, it would have been what they wanted to happen. To the rest of the world, it would have been disastrous, because few would have acquiesced to his reign.

But doing so gradually, tricking the entire population of the earth into thinking that through the New Age (and all that it entails), his "benevolence" is the very thing that this earth needs to survive, is the only way he will be able to gain access to the throne.

Remember, Nimrod was at least part human, though very well could have been one of the dreaded Nephilim. Satan worked through

Nimrod to unite all people under one banner, and that banner is simply the idea that what we can conceive, we can achieve. God of course knew that if/when humanity became one in thought there would be nothing they could not achieve. For this reason, God had to change the plan of Satan, bringing it to nothing. Why? Simply because Jesus had not been born, had not lived, and had not yet died and rose again. All of this was still into the far future. Time needed to march onward until these events took place.

Now that Jesus' life, death, and resurrection is behind us on the timeline, God is going to allow Satan to do what he can in his upcoming attempt to overthrow God. God will actually give Satan nearly free reign to do what he wants and needs to do to accomplish his plan.

Satan knows he must trick humanity into thinking that he is the true benevolent king, coming to free humanity from the dictates of the antiquated ways wrapped up in biblical thinking. It will read like Romans chapter one where Paul tells us of the downward spiral that human beings of the past took when they wanted nothing more to do with God at all. Finally, God gives them (literally *throws them*) over to their own desires, giving up on attempting to save them from themselves.

People will look forward to the alleged redemption that Satan will attempt to foist on unsuspecting humanity through his son, the Antichrist. They will follow him with unbending loyalty, blind to the fact that he is the *liar of liars*.

Aliens have come of age. They are not only here to stay but their influence is *growing*. Not long after the earthquake and resultant tsunami wiped out much of northern Japan, a UFO was allegedly seen hovering over the damaged nuclear reactor. Was it real? Who knows, but it was widely reported in various news sources. The photo on the next page highlights the event in question. If it was real,

ALIENology

why did a UFO choose the nuclear reactor to hover near? The number of UFO sightings has increased a great deal over the past number of decades.

Anyone within the UFO field of study will tell you that Israel has always been a hotbed of UFO activity, and the number of sightings has increased as well over the past few decades.

It seems as though Satan is preparing to make his greatest reveal soon in the form of extra-terrestrial life. Aliens are already accepted as superior in intelligence and technology. Their alleged technology is far more advanced than anything we have today.

Aliens appear willing to share that knowledge, even if it is largely religious at the moment. They seem benevolent, though not to everyone. They appear to be waiting in the wings so as not to create undue panic and fear. They say they want to help and they appear to

exhibit an endless supply of patience toward humanity.

Of course, things are not always what they appear to be, and we have only their word to go by if we choose to ignore the Bible. The question then becomes: what will you do about the subject of aliens? Will you believe what they transmit to a plethora of human beings who tell us that they are here to help and only have our best interests at heart? Will you believe that or will you look deeper, beyond the façade, to try to determine what they are really about?

Please do not close this book without reading the last chapter. It may make the difference between life and death, believing a lie or seeing the truth. Please read on.

16

What About You?

Do you know when you will die? Are you aware of the day and hour when you will slip from this life into eternity? I bet you do not know when that will happen. So why are you living as if you **_do_** know when it will happen? Putting a decision about Jesus off until another day is taking a huge chance because of the fact that you do not know when you will die. That is plainly simple, and logic alone demands that you do not put this decision off. Yet you do, because the thought of becoming a Christian makes you feel uncomfortable.

You wrongly believe that to become a Christian means that you have to change in a major way *before* Jesus will accept you. It means to you giving up the things you love now because if you love them, then obviously they are wrong and God does not love them.

You are putting the cart before the horse. You must understand that God is not rejecting you. He is not standing there, tapping His foot, demanding that you eliminate those things that He does not like before you can come to Him for salvation.

If you (or anyone) could do that, you would not *need* His salvation at all. It is because you and I do things that are not pleasing to Him that we need His salvation.

What do you do that you would like to no longer do? Do you drink excessively until you cannot control it? Do you play around with drugs? Do you eat too much food until you have become overweight, lethargic and sickly?

What other things are in your life that you do not like? Are you drawn to illicit extra-marital affairs? Do you have a problem with lust? Are you a shopaholic? Do you tend to tell lies a great deal because it makes you feel important, or to hide things about your life?

Do you find that you do not like people and you would prefer to be around animals or out in the woods than around people? Are you a workaholic? Do you place a high value on money and you find that you work very hard to obtain it?

Here's the problem. The enemy of our souls comes to us and tells us that God will never accept us until we get rid of those things. He lies to us that God essentially wants us "perfect" before He will be willing to meet us and grant us eternal life. This is completely untrue.

The other lie that our enemy tells us is that we should not become a Christian because the fun in our life will fly out the door. We will no longer be able to drink or do the fun things we enjoy now. We start to think that coming to God means becoming a doormat for people and having to fill our life with things we do not want to *ever* do.

These are all lies, and unfortunately, too many people believe them. First of all, God does not expect you to be "perfect" before you come to Him for salvation. If that were the case, no one would be able to ever approach Him.

Secondly, God does not say that He is going to take away all the things we enjoy and replace them with things we hate. What is wrong with enjoying the lake on your boat? What is wrong with spending a day with the family fishing or just relaxing in the mountains? There is nothing wrong with these things.

What God *will* do is begin to remove the things that have ensnared you so that life is actually draining from you, but you are not aware of it. For instance, maybe you drink excessively and you have tried everything you can think of to quit. You have gone to AA meetings, spent thousands of dollars on this program or that, and you have even used your own will power to free yourself from the addiction to alcohol, all to no avail.

The question is not: *do I need to quit before I come to Jesus?* The question is: *am I willing to allow Him to work in and through me to take away the addiction I have to alcohol?* Do you see the difference? Are you willing to allow Him to work in you to break that addiction so that you will become a healthier person, one who is able to think straight and one who learns to rely on Him for strength? That is all He wants you to be able to do. He knows you cannot break that addiction (or any addiction for that matter) with your own strength and willpower. Are you willing to allow Him to do it in and through you?

What if you are a workaholic? What if you have "things" like a boat, a house in Cancun, a large bank account, four cars, and more? Do you think that God is going to ask you to give it up, or worse, do you think that God will simply come in and take all of that from you? I know of nothing in Scripture that tells us He will do that.

What God will do with all of those who come to Him trusting Him for salvation is one thing, which begins the moment we receive salvation and will continue until the day we stand before Him. He will begin to create within us the character of Jesus (cf. Ephesians 2:10).

Here is a verse from the Old Testament that was said originally through the prophet Ezekiel to the people of Israel. While this was specifically stated to the Jews, it is applicable to all who receive salvation through Jesus Christ.

"I will give you a new heart and put a new spirit within you; I will take the heart of stone out of your flesh and give you a heart of flesh. I will put My Spirit within you and cause you to walk in My statutes, and you will keep My judgments and do them" (Ezekiel 36:26-27).

God is speaking here through Ezekiel, and He is saying that He will give the people a new heart of flesh, removing that old heart of stone. This is God's responsibility. God is the One who makes that happen. We are told in the book of Hebrews that God is the Author and Finisher of our faith (cf. Hebrews 12:2). This tells me that God is the One who changes me from within so that over time, my desires are slowly turned into His desires.

I recall years ago thinking that God wanted to do everything in my life that I did not want Him to do. I fell into the asinine belief that He wanted to change everything about me. What I learned is that yes, there are things that God does want to change about me. However, there is a lot that God originally gave me that He has also enhanced and used for His glory.

Maybe you are a workaholic who thinks that working hard is something God does not want you to do. This is not necessarily the case. He may have given you the ability and the knowledge to work in the area of finance for a great purpose. All He may wind up doing is dialing back your workaholic tendencies so that you have more time to enjoy your family and study His Word.

But you say you smoke, or drink, or use illegal drugs, and you don't want to give those up. As I stated, you can't give those up under your own power, and the fact that you have tried so many times has proven it to you.

But God knows what is and what is not good for you. Are you willing to *allow* Him to work in you to change your desires so that you no longer want to smoke, use illegal drugs, or drink nearly as much?

Then you say that you believe God wants to make you a Christian so you can become miserable. Isn't that what most Christians are; miserable? Not the Christians I know, and certainly not me, my wife, or our children.

Where does the Bible say that God wants us miserable? You will not find it. What God wants is for us to be blessed, and that begins when we receive salvation from His hand.

You know, if we would stop and take the time to consider the fact that this life is exceedingly short if we compare it to eternity, we will then realize that there is nothing so important that it should keep us from receiving Jesus as Savior and Lord.

Unfortunately, too many people do not consider the brevity of life. They think they will live forever, or at the very least, they will die when they are really old and gray. That will come too soon. This author is going to be 54 years old in just a few months from this writing. It truly seems like yesterday that I was a young boy fishing in the Delaware River near Hobart, New York. There I spent many Saturdays fishing and simply enjoying being outdoors. How did life go by so very quickly? How could that have happened?

It has happened, and I am at a point in life where not only do I realize that this life is short, but I actually look forward to spending eternity with Jesus after this life. Does that sound morbid to you? It shouldn't, because by comparing this life to eternity, we should get a sense of what is truly important.

God does not expect us to become Mother Theresas. He does not necessarily expect us to give up everything and become missionaries in outer Mongolia. What God expects is for us to simply allow Him to change our character as He sees fit.

Over time, we may well find that we have simply stopped swearing without realizing it. Our desire for cigarettes or alcohol has nearly evaporated. Illicit affairs no longer enter the picture.

We also may find that some of the things we want to eliminate in our life become more pronounced. Often the enemy will do this to cause us to focus on something that God is not even doing in our lives at that point. It causes tension, frustration, and self-anger.

If you have gotten to this point in your life and you have not dealt with the question about Jesus, it is about time you do so. You need to stop what you are doing and realize a couple of things before you go through another minute in this life.

- **Sinner**: you need to realize that you are a sinner. You have sinned and you will continue to sin. Sin is breaking the laws that God has set up. We all sin. We have all broken God's laws and that breaks any connection we might have had with God. Sin pushes us away from Him.

    Romans 3:23 says *"For all have sinned, and come short of the glory of God."* That means you and that means me. All means all. That is the first step. We need to recognize and agree with God that yes, we are sinners. I'm a sinner. You are a sinner. This results in God's anger, what the Bible terms "wrath."

- **God's Wrath**: Romans 1:18 says, *"For the wrath of God is revealed from heaven against all ungodliness and unrighteousness of men, who suppress the truth in unrighteousness."*

This is as much a fact as the truth that we are all sinners. Because we are sinners – by breaking God's law(s) – God has every right to be angry with us and ultimately destroy that which is sinful. If we choose to remain "in" our sinful states throughout this life, we will – unfortunately – be destroyed with the rest of sin.

Fortunately, there *is* a remedy, and it is salvation.

- **God's Gift**: In the sixteenth chapter of Acts, a jailer asks Paul this famous question: *what must I do to be saved?* The question was asked because Paul and Barnabas had been imprisoned, and while there, they began singing praises to God.

God then sent a powerful earthquake that opened the doors to all the prison cells, yet no one escaped. When the jailer arrived, he saw that everyone was still in their cells, and after seeing that miracle (what prisoner would not want to escape from prison?), turned and asked what he must do to be saved. He was speaking of the spiritual aspect of things. He wanted to know how he could be guaranteed eternal life.

The answer Paul gave the man was, *"Believe on the Lord Jesus Christ, and thou shalt be saved, and thy house"* (Acts 16:31).

This is not head knowledge or intellectual assent. This is *believing from the heart.* In fact, Paul makes a very similar statement in another book he wrote, Romans. He says, *"That if thou shalt confess with thy mouth the Lord Jesus, and shalt believe in thine heart that God hath raised him from the dead, thou shalt be saved. For with the heart man believeth unto righteousness; and with the mouth confession is made unto salvation"* (Romans 10:9-10).

When we fully believe something, we confess that it is true. It must begin in the heart because that is where the will is located. We must want to believe. We must endeavor to believe. We must seek to believe.

We must stop giving ourselves all the reasons to deny or ignore Jesus. As God, He became a Man, born of a virgin. He clothed Himself with humanity that He might show us how to live, and in so doing, would keep every portion of the law.

If Jesus was capable of keeping every portion of the law, then He would be found worthy to become a sacrifice for our sin – yours and mine. If He became a sacrifice for our sin, then all that we must do is embrace Him and His sacrificial death.

In short then, to become saved we must:

1. Admit (we sin)
2. Repent (want to turn away from it)
3. Believe (that Jesus is the answer)
4. Embrace (the truth about Jesus)

We **admit** that we are sinner, that we have sinned. This is nothing more than agreeing with God that we have broken His law. Can you honestly say that you have not broken God's law? If you admit to breaking even the "smallest" law, then you are a lawbreaker.

After we admit that we have sinned, the next step is found in **repenting**. Some believe that repenting is actually moving away from sin. This author believes that it is a willingness to move away from sin, and there is a difference.

As we have already discussed, it is impossible to stop sinning. Human beings simply cannot do it because as long as we live, we will have a sin nature, which is something within us that gives us a propensity to sin. As long as we have this inner propensity to sin or break God's laws, we will never be perfect in this life.

We cannot one day say "Lord, I promise to stop sinning." If we do that, we are only kidding ourselves and setting ourselves up for major failure. We cannot stop sinning in this life. The most we can do is *want* to stop sinning and then spend the rest of our lives allowing God to create the character of Jesus within us, slowly, little by little.

Repenting is to decide that you no longer want to do the things that keep us out of heaven. We no longer wish to break God's laws. It is not promising God that we will never sin again.

Once we admit, then repent, we must **believe**. This is one of the most difficult things to do because believing that Jesus died in our place, that He lived a perfectly sinless life, is extremely difficult to believe. Our minds cannot grasp that truth. We must ask God to open our eyes to that truth so that we can embrace it.

While on the cross next to Jesus, the one thief joined the other thief in ridiculing Jesus. Then, all of a sudden – as we read in Luke 23 – this same thief that had just been ridiculing Him now turned to Him with a new understanding.

It was this new understanding that prompted the thief to say to Jesus, *"Lord, remember me when you come into your Kingdom."* Jesus looked at the man and responded to him, *"Today, you will be with me in paradise."*

What had occurred in the mind and heart of that thief from one moment to the next? One thing, and that one thing was that God opened the thief's eyes so that he could see the truth. It was as if the blinders fell off and he now saw and understood who Jesus was, even to the most cursory degree that Jesus was dying not for Himself, but for others.

It was this understanding, this awareness, which prompted the man to ask Jesus to simply be remembered. Jesus went way beyond it to promise the man that he would be with Jesus that day in paradise.

Please notice in Luke 23 that there is nothing in the chapter that tells us that the man promised Jesus he would give up sin, or that he would never sin again. There is nothing that tells us that thief took the time to enter into a final deathbed confession of his sins so that he could be absolved.

The thief made no promises to Jesus at all. What he experienced was the truth of who Jesus was and what Jesus accomplished for humanity. Jesus accomplished what we cannot. What is left is for each person to *admit, repent, believe,* and *embrace*.

Let me clarify here that though we do not see any verbal repentance from the thief, we know that he did repent. He admitted as well. How can we know this? Because of the thief's complete about-face with respect to his attitude toward Jesus. One minute, he was ridiculing Jesus, and the next, embracing Him. This is important. There is no way he could have or would have *embraced* Jesus had he not been humbled by the truth *about* Jesus.

Once the thief saw the truth, he was instantly humbled. Within himself, he knew that he was a sinner, and in fact the text states that this is what he told the other thief dying next to him. *"But the other answering rebuked him, saying, Dost not thou fear God, seeing thou art in the same condemnation? And we indeed justly; for we receive the due reward of our deeds: but this man hath done nothing amiss"* (Luke 23:40-41). Something happened within the heart of the one thief. In one moment, the thief went from harassing Jesus to recognizing his own sinfulness, and then ultimately, asking for grace, which was freely given to him.

Whether he said it or not, the thief went from haughtiness to humility in a very short space of time, and it was all because he saw the truth about Jesus. That truth helped him realize that he deserved his death and what would happen to him after death. He understood that Jesus did not deserve death.

From here, the thief fully embraced the truth about Jesus and was rewarded with eternal life because of it. He did not come off the cross to be water baptized. He did not list a long litany of offenses against God. He recognized the truth about Jesus, was humbled, and embraced that truth!

This is what each of us needs to do. We cannot give in to the lie that tells us that we are not good enough, or we have not given up enough before God will accept us. We must reject the lie that says we must somehow earn our salvation.

Jesus has done everything that is necessary to make salvation available to us. The only thing that is left for us is to see the truth. Once we see that truth, it should humble us to the point of embracing Jesus and all that He stands for and is to us.

The eighth chapter of Romans begins with the fact that all who trust Jesus for salvation are no longer condemned...*ever.* All of my sins –

past, present, and future – have not only been forgiven, but canceled. It is because of my faith in the atonement (death) of Jesus that God is able to cancel all of my sins, even the ones that I have not committed yet. This does not make me eager to commit them. It makes me want to do what I can to avoid sinning.

If you do not know Jesus, please do not put down this book without deliberately *believing* that He is God, that He died for you by the shedding of His blood on the cross, and that He rose three days later because death could not keep Him. Do you believe that? If you do not yet believe it, do you *want* to believe it? If so, then simply ask God to help you come to believe all that Jesus is and all that He has accomplished for you. God will answer your prayers and you may either receive instantaneous awareness of all that Jesus is and has done, or it may be a *growing* awareness over time. In either case, it is the most important decision you will ever make.

Turn to Him now and pray for knowledge of the truth and an ability to embrace it. Please. He is waiting for you.

Ask Yourself:

1. Do you *know* Jesus? Are you in *relationship* with Him? Have you had a spiritual transaction according to John 3?
2. Do you *want* to receive eternal life through the only salvation that is available?
3. Do you believe that Jesus is God the Son, who was born of a virgin, lived a sinless life, died a bloody and gruesome death to pay for your sin, was buried, and rose again on the third day? Do you *believe* this?
4. Do you *want* to *embrace* the truth from #3?
5. Pray that God will open your eyes and provide you with the faith to begin believing the truth about Jesus. Ask Him to help your faith embrace the truth, realizing that you are not good enough to save yourself and that your sin will keep you out of God's Kingdom without His salvation.

ALIENology

6. Pray as if your life depended upon it because *it does*!
7. If you have prayed to receive Jesus as Savior and Lord, please write to me. I want to send you some materials at *no charge or obligation*. Write to me at **fred_deruvo@hotmail.com** and sign up for our free bimonthly newsletter at **www.studygrowknow.com**

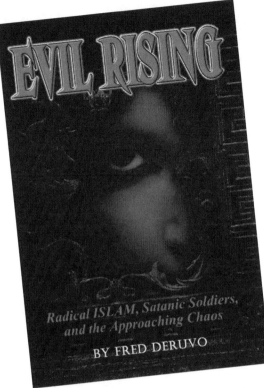

There is a chaos coming that is predicated upon the rise of Islam, Satanic Soldiers, aliens, and evil beyond measure. As an ideology, Islam masquerades as a religious light to the world, one that promises to usher in world peace; but at what cost? Through the use of political strategies, military might, and religious tenets, adherents of Islam work within various established governments to create special laws or exemptions for Muslims in the hope of eventually overthrowing that established government. Can it happen? IS it happening? Find out in *Evil Rising*. ($13.95; 184 pages, 978-0977424429)

We hear all the time how bad things are getting throughout the world. Do we chalk it all up to being the normal cycles that occur in life, or is something else going on behind the scenes? What if this generation alive now turns out to be the last one before Jesus returns? Is there any truth at all to the claim that Jesus will return one day? If you are one who has not taken the time to read through some of the books of the Bible that are said to teach truths regarding the last days, *Living in the Last Generation* puts it out there in a straightforward manner, making it easy to understand. ($11.95; 132 pages, ISBN: 978-0977424405)

Made in the USA
Charleston, SC
24 October 2011